REFUGEE WORLD

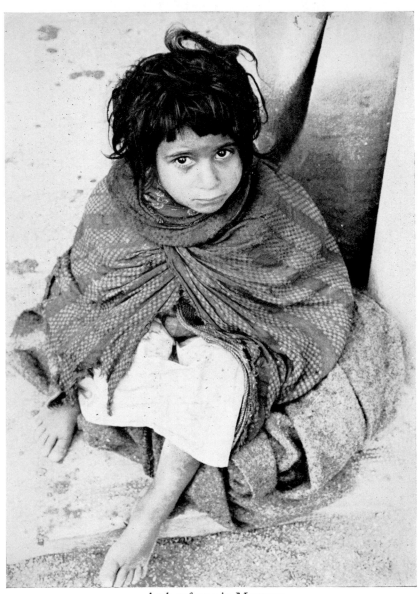

Arab refugee in Morocco

Refugee World

ROBERT KEE

LONDON
OXFORD UNIVERSITY PRESS
NEW YORK TORONTO
1961

Oxford University Press, Amen House, London E.C.4

GLASGOW NEW YORK TORONTO MELBOURNE WELLINGTON
BOMBAY CALCUTTA MADRAS KARACHI KUALA LUMPUR
CAPE TOWN IBADAN NAIROBI ACCRA

© Robert Kee 1961

PRINTED IN GREAT BRITAIN

CONTENTS

ILLUSTRATIONS

PREFACE

In July 1960 I made a tour of some of the refugee areas of Germany and Austria to see how the end of World Refugee Year left the refugees themselves. This book is mainly an account of that journey. But I should like to emphasize here that the refugee situation in Europe is only one very small example of the total world refugee problem. Like a terrible disease which leaves its marks on the patient long after the climax is past, the refugee problem in Europe appears slowly to be coming to an end. How slowly this report will show. But in other refugee situations which involve very many more human beings, there is no prospect whatever of an end. And in our world a completely new refugee situation may develop almost anywhere at any time. The suffering that comes from being uprooted from home by fear and the call on our sense of responsibility is, in our time, continuous. Because the refugee situation in Germany and Austria today illustrates so much of what should and should not have been done, so much success and so much failure, it may perhaps serve better than any other both as an inspiration and a warning. For refugee situations are today as much a permanent feature of our civilization as was, in the Middle Ages, the plague.

In the course of the investigations for this book I have seen many people, all of whom—officials, social workers, and refugees—have most courteously given up their time to talk to me. Sketches of some of them appear in the text. Here I should like to thank particularly the following who went out of their way to help me, either by seeing me at short notice when they were busy or off duty, or by making invaluable arrangements for me which I could not possibly have made for myself in the time available.

Miss Janet Lacey, of the British Council of Churches
Mr. Arthur Foster, of the World Council of Churches
Miss Ella Larsen, of the International Rescue Committee
Mrs. F. C. Rigby, of the British Adoption Committee for Displaced Persons

Miss Torker, of the National Catholic Welfare Conference, Vienna

Mr. R. Watson, of the British Adoption Committee for Displaced Persons, Munich

Mr. J. Lebidev, of the Tolstoy Foundation, Munich

Mr. Michael Rudko, of the United Ukrainian Relief Committee, Munich

Mr. Ahmed Balagiya, of Jamat Al' Islam (Muslim Refugee Agency)

Mr. Roger Walon, of the Intergovernmental Committee for European Migration, Salzburg

Mr. Paul Kelly, United States Escapee Programme, Salzburg

Herr Werner Middelmann, Director of the Federal Ministry for Refugees, Bonn

Dr. August Lindt, former United Nations High Commissioner for Refugees

Mr. V. Tedesco, of the United Nations High Commissioner's Office, Geneva

Mrs. Sophie Lennox, of the United Nations High Commissioner's Office, Bonn

Mr. William McCoy, of the United Nations High Commissioner's Office, Vienna

I am particularly indebted to these last three members of the High Commissioner's staff who gave up their leisure to attend to my insistent and often critical demands. Except for opinions specifically attributed to individuals, none of the opinions or conclusions expressed in this book is of course, anybody's but my own.

GREAT BEDWYN, 1961

Perchance he for whom this bell tolls, may be so ill, as that he knows not it tolls for him. . . . No man is an island, entire of itself; every man is a piece of the continent, a part of the main; if a clod be washed away by the sea, Europe is the less, as well as if a promontory were, as well as if a manor of thy friends or of thine own were; any man's death diminishes me, because I am involved in mankind. . . .

JOHN DONNE. Devotions XVII

World Refugee Year has *not* solved the refugee problem.

JAMES J. NORRIS
President of the International
Catholic Migration Commission

November 1960

INTRODUCTION

A good deal of the writing about the world's refugee situation today makes the ordinary reader rub his eyes in bewilderment. Is it himself, he wonders, or the writer who is thus apparently rendering down the strong bones of his native language into opaque soap? *'The prime force in determining the shape of the program was the group of agencies participating. The overall responsibility of the High Commissioner notwithstanding. . . .'*[1] Programmes are submitted and implemented; contributions (pledged and paid) are subjected to breakdown. The brave, unfortunate, difficult, noble, and very ordinary human beings who are the refugees are lumped together into the 'case-load', and their removal from a filthy, overcrowded hut to shelter considered fit for human beings is disguised as 'milieu therapy'.

Only the occasional unexpectedly plain statement in some official report jerks the mind back into recollection of what all this, in ordinary reader's terms, is really about.

'In view of the conditions in which most of the refugees are living—to a large extent in very exposed areas at high altitude or in desert land with only primitive shelter—second priority had to be given to the procurement of clothing, cloth and blankets. Although arrangements for the procurement of these items were made in the summer of 1959, the actual arrival of shipments was in some cases not timely enough to coincide with the onset of winter.'[2]

In other words, a number of Algerian Arabs in Tunisia and Morocco froze to death.

Yet the language of the administrators should not be derided. Abstraction is the human mind's method of dealing with problems that are otherwise too vast to deal with, and it is the job of the people who write these reports

[1] *Final Report on the Ford Foundation Programme for Refugees, primarily in Europe*, p. 21.

[2] *Report on the Implementation of General Assembly Resolutions 1286 (XIII) and 1389 (XIV) on Assistance to Refugees from Algeria in Tunisia and Morocco*, paragraph 8.

and for whom they are written to deal with the vast problem of the world's refugees. Paradoxically, though, in making it possible for themselves to deal with it they also make their task more difficult. For such language makes the problem seem remote and unreal to the man in the street without whose support it can never be dealt with effectively.

The refugee problem can only be dealt with effectively if the man in the street can see that it is not just an international administrator's or charitable organization's problem but his own. The bell which tolls for each child who starves in the streets of Calcutta or on the roof-tops of Hong Kong, or for each elderly Pole or Balt or Yugoslav who kills himself out of despair in one of the rejected corners of Europe, tolls for each one of us. And this is true both in the sense that we share a common humanity with all other men, a part of each one of us living and dying in each other, and also in a narrower, more practical sense; for the world has now become so small that misery in one part of it can very soon have disastrous repercussions over the whole.

In the spring of 1959, the year in which the Russians succeeded in photographing the other side of the moon and in which the majority of the Western world 'never had it so good', a Columbian Father returning from a visit to refugees on some of the islands off the south-west coast of Korea reported: 'I have been all around this area. There not only is no food in the houses. There is no moss left on the rocks.'[5] At about the same time a Pakistan Government official was investigating the housing of some of the 500,000 Muslim refugees living in Karachi. In his report he wrote that the average family of four persons was living in space that would have been considered insufficient for two water buffalo. He added: 'Even the earliest human dwellings discovered by archeologists were bigger and more comfortable than the ones we had the painful duty to survey.'[6]

[5] See *World Refugee Year*, published by the International Catholic Migration Council, p. 54.

[6] Statement made by Mr. M. S. M. Baig, Ambassador of Pakistan to Austria, Switzerland, and Yugoslavia in Geneva, March 1960.

It is not just money that is needed. Although, of course, nothing can be done without money, this is in one way the least important necessity. The amount of money needed to deal with the refugee problem is something far greater than could ever go under the name of charity or than could be contributed by individuals acting as individuals. What is needed is a fresh approach to responsibility, and for this there must be knowledge and understanding.

Geneva, headquarters of the United Nations High Commissioner for Refugees and his considerable staff headquarters also of several Christian and humanitarian organizations for the welfare of refugees, is not the best place in which to learn about refugees. Here in summer the chestnut trees and the roses, the lush grass, the buttercups and the lilac in which the Palais des Nations lies embedded overpurify the air of the world. Here the peacocks stroll. Here there are times when the most human things seem the faces of the pansies in the flower-beds. Here someone working for refugees, to whom in May 1960 I put the question, 'What is your biggest problem at the moment?' replied: 'Quite frankly, how I'm going to spend nearly a million dollars on refugees by Christmas!'

At least he was being honest. It wasn't his fault that the administrative machinery for helping refugees was so complex that he was largely absorbed by its technical manipulation. But I was to remember the remark later in damp wooden barracks in Germany and Austria where behind thin, rotting partitions, families of five or six slept, cooked, ate, and washed in gloomy rooms which for years they had tried to keep neat and gay while they waited 'under the mandate of the High Commissioner'.

You can learn at Geneva about this mandate and about the theory of the refugee world almost as if it were an academic subject, like metaphysics or the natural sciences. But to the refugee himself all this bears little relation to the reality he knows. For an effective understanding of the refugee problem, it is the refugee's own world that counts, and that is not at all a neat or logical place, however hard people may work to try to make it seem so. The refugee knows a bewildering, frustrating world full of remote chances, humiliation, emotion, squalor, dignity, disappointment, and hope. He may of necessity acquire some of the jargon on which his destiny hangs, but he will never think of himself as most of the people dealing with him do, as just an individual part of a case-load. To be a refugee means to smell certain smells, to share a water-tap with dozens of other people, to sleep in overcrowded rooms, to hear noises day and night through thin walls, to be doing all this for years, perhaps, in a community of people who once used you as a slave, to know perhaps that you will never again hear your mother tongue spoken by most of the people among whom you live, to worry about your wife and children doing these things too, and to worry also, like anyone else, about how to make ends meet.

This world in which the refugee lives is called 'the field' by the denizens of the paper world of Geneva. With its connotation of air and light and fresh greenness, the term sometimes seems subconsciously designed as yet another convenient word with which to keep reality at bay.

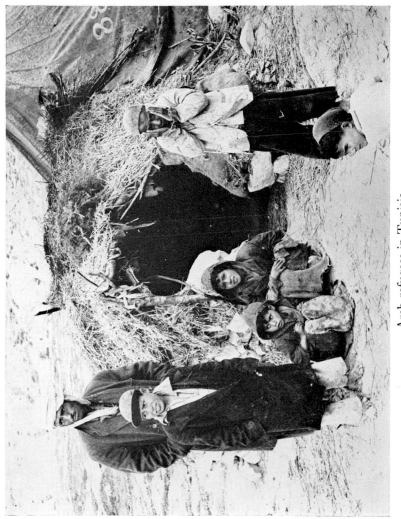

Arab refugees in Tunisia

Sophie Lennox
'You have to handle these people with velvet gloves, you know.'

Watson
'this one's not even officially an unofficial camp. . . .'

GERMANY

I

'Sophie Lennox Information Office Will Meet You Wahn Airport' the cable signed HICOMREF[1] had said. After waiting about for some time in the long hall at Wahn I went to the B.E.A. ticket counter. There was a message there telling me that I should take the bus from the airport to the air terminal. It was as if this were somehow part of the Information

Long ago I had myself worked for a short time in the Information department of an international organization and now, like the echoes of a familiar nightmare, I seemed to recognize the old, immaculate touch which signified nothing. Quickly I reproached myself with the reminder that this time I was 'in the field'.

From the windows of the moving bus, I stared at the new Luftwaffe officers walking about outside the airport in their new blue uniforms, superficially so very like their old. But the German guards on the gates wore American-style helmets and even moved loosely like Americans inside their shirt-sleeved summer outfit. I thought how very old and out-of-the-way the refugee problem in Germany seemed now and what a long, long time ago it had all started.

Into these same ex-Luftwaffe barracks in 1945 U.N.R.R.A. had probably put 'displaced persons'—those millions of slave labourers taken by the Germans from Russia, the Ukraine, Poland, and almost every other country in Europe to help build Hitler's Thousand Year Reich. Though hundreds of thousands of these had died from overwork, disease, and torture during the war, there had still been many millions left at the end of it. By the end of June 1947 U.N.R.R.A. had assisted in the repatriation of some 7,000,000 of these—of whom 6,000,000 were repatriated in the first

[1] High Commissioner for Refugees.

few months after the end of the war. But many of the
Russians and Ukrainians had been glad of the chance not
to return to a Communist régime. And citizens from other
countries such as Yugoslavia and Poland, which had become
Communist in the meantime or where the political situation
was precarious had preferred to stay where they were too—
in spite of the inducements of a sixty-day food ration which
at that time were offered by the United Nations to such
people to try and get them to return.[2] In this way perhaps
as many as 1,000,000 former D.P.s turned automatically into
refugees. They were joined by hundreds of thousands of
others, who left the new Iron Curtain countries in the
years just after the war.[3]

On 30 June 1947 the blue life-belt insignia of the International Refugee Organization (I.R.O.) replaced the red
trappings of U.N.R.R.A. on headquarter buildings, camp
gates and official vehicles. Altogether in the five years of its
existence I.R.O. registered just over 1,500,000 refugees and
succeeded in resettling 1,000,000 of them. 'You know,' a
U.S. Baptist pastor had said, addressing former D.P.s, now
refugees in a camp at Aaschaffenburg in the summer of
1947: 'You are not strangers to us. America was founded
by the voluntarily displaced. We are a nation of the displaced from all the lands, from many more than you have
represented here.'[4] It was on the basis of such sentiments
that in June 1948 Congress passed the D.P. Act, which by
January 1952 had resettled 300,000 in the United States
alone. But getting refugees through the provisions of this
Act and through the elaborate and closely worked clauses of
other countries' immigration laws had been an almost
superhuman task for the dedicated workers of I.R.O. Often

---

[2] See *The Wild Place* by Kathryn Hulme, p. 129.

[3] 'Statistical lag and discrepancies in classification from area to area
made it difficult in the period from 1945 to early 1948 to arrive at reliable
figures as to the recorded number of refugees and displaced persons.
Such figures as are available can only give some idea of the great dimen-
sions of the task. . . . The Allied military authorities estimated that by
31 December 1946 a total number of 1,037,404 displaced persons were
living in and out of camps in Germany, Austria and Italy.' *The International Refugee Organisation*, by L. W. Holborn, O.U.P., 1956, p. 188.

[4] Kathryn Hulme, op. cit., p. 165.

they had succeeded with a case only after years of disappointment and persistence. Often they had failed altogether. One chief resettlement officer worked out that the documents in the file of a single case laid end to end stretched for seventeen yards. A Ukrainian doctor who performed thirty major operations a week 'wept like a child when he was rejected from a scheme calling for hard-rock miners for Canada'.[5] A Polish Countess was delayed on 'security' grounds because she had received a degree from Leningrad University in 1910.[6] Whole refugee families had to remain in camps because one member was rejected by the immigration authorities—perhaps the father had the tops of three fingers missing, or the mother had heart trouble, or one of the children had a leg shorter than the other. Unmarried mothers and their families were disqualified and had to remain in the camps on 'social' grounds. Men who had been caught working the black market in the starvation days after the war and given short sentences were similarly rejected on 'social' grounds, and thus punished, with their families, for life for one trivial misdemeanour. A young Pole whose application for a visa to the States had been delayed over and over again was finally rejected because the daughter who had been born to him while he and his wife were waiting in a camp had contracted T.B. while waiting too. 'For the first time', wrote the I.R.O. officer for whom he had been working for years as a chauffeur, 'he looked like a real refugee'.[7]

In this way Western democratic bureaucracy created thousands and thousands of refugees as surely as did the tyranny of the Communist régimes.

In January 1952 those 300,000 still unsettled refugees who had been unable to get through the mesh of the immigration laws were labelled 'the hard core'—as if the difficulty in moving them had somehow been their own fault—and quietly abandoned. The I.R.O. was closed down and the United Nations simply appointed a High Commissioner for

[5] Kathryn Hulme, op. cit., p. 170.
[6] Kathryn Hulme, op. cit., p. 217.
[7] Op. cit., p. 232.

Refugees in Geneva, with a very small administrative staff to look after their diplomatic and legal interests. Their material welfare was declared to be the concern of those national governments on whose territory their camps and hovels were to be found.

But as has been said: 'Man is not a mathematical element about whom we can say: "If we cannot help him this year or next, we'll help him the year after." He may die in the meantime. He may lose spirit, energy, and sink into apathy. As a result of privation or near-starvation feeding, he may fall ill, or turn into an anti-social being who curses the world for letting him rot.'[8] This in fact was exactly what happened.

For some years the United Nations gave the High Commissioner no money at all with which to help materially the refugees under his mandate. The first assistance came through the benevolence of the Ford Foundation and, shamed perhaps by this example, the United Nations late in 1954 voted to the High Commissioner £6,000,000 to be spread over four years and to be spent on programmes for 'permanent solution for refugees'. It has been pointed out that this sum was less per year than the city of New York spends on keeping its streets clean and less than the British National Health Service spends on medicines in one week.[9]

It was the Hungarians fleeing from their country after the rising of 1956 who made people think seriously about refugees again. Most of these new Hungarian refugees were young, fit and active, the *élite* of a brave nation, and every country was glad to introduce the strain into its own population. Almost all the 200,000 Hungarian refugees were successfully resettled within a year. Other 'new' refugees also arrived—on a less dramatic scale than the Hungarians of 1956, but steadily all the same: 400 or so a month into Austria from Yugoslavia, about the same number into Italy, about forty-five a month into Greece, and always the occasional Czech or Pole or post-1956 Hungarian risking

[8] See H. J. Chandler, *The High Tower of Refuge* (Odhams), p. 222. Dr. Chandler is Director of the Refugee Service of the World Council of Churches.
[9] See Chandler, op. cit., p. 223.

death over the heavily patrolled and often mined or electrified frontiers.

All these 'new' refugees had received considerable help from the United States Escapee Programme, founded in 1952 for 'new' refugees exclusively, with a budget larger than the High Commissioner's. Because they had not been kept waiting for years in unhealthy camps, their chances of getting past the various immigration criteria were considerably better than those of the 'old' refugees.

So, as my airport bus moved complacently into the outskirts of the prosperous little provincial town that is the capital of the German Federal Republic, and I looked out at that prosperity which for years everybody had taken for granted, it was of the 'old' refugees that I was thinking.

For over fifteen years now they had been living in the same wooden barracks in which I myself had lived fifteen years ago as a prisoner of war. It was a fantastic thought. I wanted to jump up in my seat in the bus. There must be people who were now young adults whose only memory could be of those camps. But the bus had suddenly come to a standstill in the unpretentious bus station, as if insisting that the present is always the present and that it is a waste of time to think of it in terms of the past. A member of the High Commissioner's office was courteously waiting there to meet me.

This middle-aged, roundish, Dickensian-looking man who spoke like an Englishman and now obligingly took hold of one handle of my bag was a Canadian by birth; and his name was Mr. Roland Chaput de Saintonge. Long before the war he had been a student in Geneva. During the war he had worked in the Ministry of Information in London. After the war he had been in the Control Commission, had gone into the German section of the Foreign Office and was now Deputy Chief Information Officer of the High Commissioner's office at Geneva.

'Of course, I don't know how long this job will last,' he said—surprisingly for a man who clearly knew as much about his job as he did—over a beer and a very long sausage.

A meeting with Sophie Lennox had been arranged. There

would be sandwiches at her flat, but in the meantime it wouldn't do any harm to take a snack. We sat on a terrace under a fitfully dripping chestnut tree, watching the Bonn rush-hour tail off in the rain and he talked of refugees as if they were some commodity in which he had been dealing all his life.

A Home Office team had just been in Europe selecting families under the British Government's second World Refugee Year scheme for settling long-term cases in Britain. Although the British Council for Aid to Refugees had arranged block sponsorship for 1,000 people, in fact only some 440 cases had been accepted. Part of the reason for this was said to be that people were reluctant to leave the camps. This seemed to me to fit in oddly with the picture that had been painted of the refugees' plight in World Refugee Year publicity. But Saintonge took it in his stride.

'It's so difficult to see this sort of thing in human terms,' he said. I looked at him sharply. He didn't bat an eyelid. 'You've got to though, or you won't make any sense of it at all. These are people of flesh and blood, not just cases. They've been in camps for years and years—on and off for twenty years, some of them. They know where they are; they're adjusted to this sort of life. The women know just where they can buy the things they want and what everything should cost, and they're naturally fearful of making the move suddenly to a strange land where they don't know the language, don't know how to do the shopping, and will have to adapt themselves to a completely new way of living. Added to that, of course, they've been up before selection teams over and over again throughout the years and rejected over and over again—as many as twenty times some of them. Are you surprised that they're mistrustful and fearful and cling to the way of life they've got used to for so long?'

'No,' I said, though some of this reminded me of the talk one used to hear in the thirties about poor people only putting coals in the bath.

'You've got to remember,' continued Saintonge, 'that many of these people are very simple peasants from Eastern

Europe. They're used to primitive standards. They'd sometimes much rather live in overcrowded huts, paying eight
marks a month rent, than in a decent apartment paying a
hundred marks a month. They don't see the point. And,
talking of that, there's another reason for you why there's
not been the immediate response to this British scheme.
There wasn't nearly enough preparatory work done before
this mission. There's complete ignorance here about Britain.
All that some of these Polish peasants, for instance, have
been told about Britain is that it's a criminal offence to
beat your wife there. Well, they've always beaten their
wives and intend to go on doing so. They think it's
wrong not to.' He paused. 'There's a story told—I don't
know how true it is, of course—about a Pole who the
night before he left with his family for England beat his
wife senseless, and when reproached said that it had been
necessary, as it would have to last her the rest of her life! . . .
But I say,' He looked at his watch. 'I think we ought to get
a move on. I said we'd be there about seven-thirty. Herr
Ober! . . .'

I don't know exactly what I had expected a refugee
'field' worker with a name like Sophie Lennox to be like,
but I had some idea of a rather dour, dedicated woman,
probably in her early fifties, with very practical shoes and
strands of greying hair blowing about her unlined face.
Sophie Lennox was in her thirties, dark, nervy and house-
proud, with *Dr. Zhivago* and *The Oxford Book of English
Verse* on the sparse bookshelves of her small neat flat. She
had been born a German Jewess in Berlin, where her father
had been a prosperous, assimilated engineer. One of her
most vivid early memories was of being taken round the
smashed Jewish shops of Berlin the day after the first out-
burst of violence against the Jews there in 1933, and of
being told by her father never to forget what she saw. He
had died in a concentration camp. Her sister had survived
one. She herself had escaped from Germany before the war.
As we ate excellent cheese and ham sandwiches and drank
whisky I felt a bore continually trying to bring the subject

back to refugees while Sophie Lennox talked of her days
broadcasting allied propaganda from Jerusalem between
1940 and 1945, and particularly of the confused personal
relationships that existed there. There were obscure patches
in her career after that, but there was talk too of dead-lines
and date-lines in the curiously remote corner of journalism
that must have been the business of representing the *New
York Times* in West Africa. She had volunteered for this
job with the High Commissioner's Office and had in fact
worked for the whole of World Refugee Year without pay.
Now, with the end of that year, she had agreed to go on the
pay-roll, but dedication was clearly there, though of a more
complicated sort than I had expected, and strangely con-
cealed by a self-assertive, worldly volubility. ' . . . Of
course, it was terrifically hard work. In fact, I worked
myself into a near-nervous breakdown in the first ten months.
Raymond Terrillon, that's our boss here, took one look at
me and said: "For God's sake, go on leave!" . . .'
Later in the evening there was a story of a courtly kiss
from Yul Brynner after a hard day's work on a film about
refugees. Clumsily, I tried to snatch at the excuse to ask
some questions, but it was late, as someone pointed out,
and we agreed to meet again the next morning. ' . . . We
start at the office at nine,' said Sophie Lennox. 'But allow
me the academic quarter of an hour, won't you?'

I allowed Sophie Lennox her academic quarter of an
hour, but when I arrived she and Saintonge were already in
her office discussing the best thing to do with a camp once
you had cleared it.
'Of course,' she explained to me, 'Burning sounds all
very well, but it's a terrible waste of money really. The
trouble is, if you sell the barracks they're used as often as
not for the erection of sub-standard housing and then
leased to new German refugees or just to the poor.'
'I did arrange for a sort of symbolic burning once,' said
Saintonge. 'Of course, I knew the Germans were too material-
istic to agree to anything like that, so I fixed it up in Austria.
But there were a lot of complaints.'

We got down to the question of who I ought to see and when. First of all there was the quite separate problem of the Germans' own 'national' refugees. An appointment had been made for me with Herr Middelmann, Director of the Federal Republic's Ministry for Refugees and Expellees. Then there appeared to be a difficulty about how soon I could visit the 'foreign' refugee camps near Stuttgart, where the greatest concentration was to be found, or when I should go to Munich, where most of the 'out-of-camp' so called 'free-livers' lived.

'You see, it's very awkward that you've come so close to the week-end.'

'But the refugees will still be there at the week-end.'

'Yes; but they're awfully touchy about people coming round and looking at them. They've had so many people in World Refugee Year.'

An issue of protocol seemed to be involved.

'You have to handle these people with velvet gloves, you know.'

'Which people?'

'They're not our camps, you see. You have to approach them through the German *Land*[10] governments.'

'Well, couldn't I speak to the *Land* government?'

'You have to approach them *through* us.'

'Well, couldn't I do that?'

'It's so close to the week-end.'

Fortunately, Sophie Lennox was as competent at dissolving difficulties as she was at conjuring them up. Soon she was on the telephone making arrangements with the electric efficiency of a good travel agent. There was only one piece of protocol she rightly insisted on, and that was that I should go and see her 'boss' first.

Raymond Terrillon, the representative of the United Nations High Commissioner for Refugees in Germany, was a dynamic thirty-seven-year-old ex-*Maquis* type of Frenchman of the modern school, broad and protein-filled, with brown hair *en brosse*, and unbelievably well-dressed in the sort of French dark suit that might also be American. His

[10] Provincial.

shirt was so white I stared in wonder at the cuffs. I felt at once that I was on the diplomatic level, and he instantly relaxed with all the unstuffy charm of the modern diplomat.

The refugees with whom he was almost entirely concerned were, he said, the old former D.P. refugees. 'They've been here for years and *years* now.' It was as if all the exasperation which they themselves were now too tired to feel was expressing itself through him. 'It's *terrible*. It's time it was finished. And it's our fault, you know. The West's. I.R.O. simply washed their hands of these people in 1952—pretended they didn't exist. It was like the ostrich.'

He reckoned that he had now about 9,000 foreign refugees in camps in Germany, and about 15,000 to 20,000 out of camp of whom perhaps 2,500 live in 'unofficial' camps. He talked, again with feeling, of the paralysing effect of the camp atmosphere after all these years.

'It really is difficult for some of them to get out now. After all, they know where they are—this is their security. They have their camp administration, their little parcels of cheese, you know. . . . They don't want to get out into the rough world.'

It was as if for a moment he was snugly in there with them. But then, talking of the various criteria which different countries still laid down for refugee immigrants, he grew angry again. 'It's such an absurd thing—this incredible time-wasting business of trying to make out which criteria are laid down by which country and then seeing which refugee can pass which. You've no idea how complicated it can be. It slows everything up *so much*. Why can't they simply let us make out a complete inventory of every refugee with his or her defect—whatever it is—his wife has a patch on her lung—or the girl is an unmarried mother—or his arm is chopped off here, or here'—and he chopped viciously at his own arm with the side of his hand once above and once below the elbow—'and then let us send this round to governments, and they could simply select whoever suited them.'

I said: 'But there are relatively so few of them now—surely it would be possible for countries to agree to share out all who are left between them. I mean waive *all* criteria.'

He raised his large hands in a traditional Gallic gesture, dropped them and smiled sadly.

'Of course, people in immigration departments like their jobs, you know . . .'

'What about you? You people will lose yours if you get on with it all too quickly.'

'We wouldn't mind. Really. We'd be delighted.' It was clear that he believed himself. 'I've seen too much of this. I've been seeing refugees ever since 1945, when I went into Austria with Military Government. And I can tell you it's awful for me that they should still be there.'

I got up. He was a convincing ambassador. As I was going out he asked his secretary to look out a file for me.

'Have a glance through it if you have the time. You'll see the sort of thing I mean. It's just one of thousands.'

And his secretary handed me the story of Dushan Dokić.

II

The covers of the file were humdrum enough, well thumbed and often pulled-out and replaced. Inside, a sheet of paper gave a few humdrum particulars of Mr. Dokić's life.

He was born in Mostar, Serbia (now part of Yugoslavia), in 1892. He had had two wives. What had happened to his first wife was not clear, but a son by this first marriage emigrated from a refugee camp to Australia in the nineteen-forties. Dushan Dokić himself came to Germany as a prisoner in August 1941. He spoke excellent German and had previously in civilian life been a skilled technician in an iron foundry. His second wife, born in 1915, had been deported to Germany in October 1941. His four children by this second marriage were now thirteen, twelve, eleven, and nine years of age.

The file itself opened in mystery with a scribbled internal note of the office of the United Nations High Commissioner

for Refugees, saying that a Mr. Lewis (who soon turned out
to be the Deputy Chief Migration Officer at the Australian
Embassy) was '. . . very understanding and promised to
see that a nice letter was written to Mr. Dokić saying that
they would be glad to consider his case. It was apparently
a security case. . . .'

It soon transpired from further letters that Terrillon had
raised Dokić's case with the Australians after meeting him
on a visit to Landshut Refugee Camp and also after Dokić
had written to the *Innere Mission*, Munich, an important
German voluntary agency working for refugees.

Following the note about Mr. Lewis's attitude, Terrillon
had written personally to Dokić on 28 December 1959 telling
him the matter was being taken up with the Australians.
Then on 6 January 1960 the real story begins to unfold.

On this date there is a letter from Dokić himself in clear,
neat handwriting on grey, lined paper. He writes in excellent
German to say that he's heard from a Mr. Winterbottom
(of the Australian Embassy) with a yellow form, *but* 'times
have now completely changed and propaganda is no longer
of any avail. I would rather have a bird in the hand than a
kangaroo in the Australian bush. I am sure that this whole
immoral bureaucratic hermaphroditism and its bestial sport
with helpless refugee families will soon find an echo in the
outside world, so that in World Refugee Year itself this other
wretched side of the refugee problem shall receive the
publicity it deserves.' The letter is very friendly to Terrillon
personally, and in it Dokić thanks Terrillon for the com-
pliment of saying that he hopes to see him again and have
a chat with him from time to time.

Enclosed with this letter to Terrillon is Dokić's answer
to the Australian Embassy, in which he says he has an
affidavit for migration to Australia which his son sent him
in 1948. He says he was originally registered for migration
in Rutzbach (Hessen) by the Australian Commission and
that 'a swindler and professional criminal by the name of
Bozidar s. Kostic' informed against him, saying that he was
a Communist: as a result he was refused a visa. All appeals,
he says, including appeals from his son in Australia, were

rejected. His request for another interview was turned down, although in May 1950 he says he appeared before the Australian Commission at Funkkaserne Munich and was treated 'like criminals are treated in prison . . .'

'Embittered [he writes], because of such inhuman treatment, I decided to stay in Germany. . . . I should like to emphasize that it would be beneath my dignity to migrate to a country where the authorities believe a criminal more than an entire family, which has every proof that they are decent people. . . . I beg to ask you to think about my case. I have been condemned without having been heard. Because of this attitude of the Australian Embassy I have lost ten years of my working life; my family has been torn apart. All this has been based on human rights, Christian faith, morals and democracy.'

As the Australian Deputy Migration Officer, Lewis, now comments: 'It would appear that nothing further could be done in the matter.'

Terrillon writes back to Dokić a friendly letter saying that he thinks that no one would hold his decision to stay in Germany against him, since so much time has passed since he first expressed his wish to emigrate. He adds that the Office of the High Commissioner is doing everything it can to see that he gets out of the camp in which he has spent so many years as soon as possible.

There then appears some new factual information about the present position of the Dokić family. Their income is 344.67 marks a month (about £30), which is made up of Dokić's pension plus children's allowance and a sum from the German Welfare Office. They were offered three rooms with kitchen and bath in a refugee settlement block of apartments at Würzburg on 19 June 1959. Dokić, however, refused to leave Landshut Camp, saying that he wanted his family to be right away from refugees when they did leave. Even within camp he keeps his children segregated from the others. He makes them kiss his hand when they leave the room, in the old Serbian custom. He is a 60 per cent. invalid.

The integration 'counsellor' of the *Innere Mission*, the

voluntary agency with which the family is registered, and the deputy camp leader at Landshut add further details. In the camp the family is housed in one large room and a small room. These are very primitive, but the rooms are kept neat and in a decent condition. Dokić is afraid of the bad influence which some elements in camp might be having on his children. This is the reason he has turned down several offers of a flat in a new housing block for refugees. He wants to be accommodated separately. There had once been a question of the family migrating to Holland, but this had fallen through like the Australian proposition.

The next item, contained in some inter-office memoranda, refers to a possibility that has come up of the Tolstoy Foundation looking after some of the children's expenses by an education grant. They could apply for a *Patenschaft* Adoption from the Save the Children Fund. The only alternative help suggested is that the three younger children should go to England under the Pestalozzi scheme, but Terrillon's office does not think this a good idea.

On 6 May 1960 Terrillon again writes to Dokić. He says that he has reason to hope that it will soon prove possible to find a private apartment for him in the centre of Land-shut—that's to say, not with the other apartment blocks destined for refugees. A representative of his has been having talks with the Bavarian Ministry of Labour about this and he (Terrillon) thinks that it will soon work out this way. He says that there's a chance of three of his children being cared for by the Tolstoy Foundation, though assistance would only cover clothing and other necessities, but not school fees. He says there was a chance too of sending three of his children to a Pestalozzi school in England but he doesn't think it would be a good solution to break the family up.

Then comes a letter dated 11 May and headed ADOPTION COMMITTEE FOR AID TO DISPLACED PERSONS, 227 Edgware Road, W.2. It is addressed to Terrillon. First, it says that entries have been received from three of the Dokić children for the Christmas Card Competition; that there wasn't much hope of their winning a prize, but that they'd receive a small consolation. It goes on to say that the money necessary to provide a flat for the Dokić family has been raised through ' . . . a friend of Mrs. Atkinson of our Berkshire branch and this group will take an interest in the family'. A copy of a reminder to the Bürgermeister of Landshut about the flat promised away from the other refugee projects accompanies the grateful reply to the Adoption Committee for Aid to Displaced Persons.

Next comes an item quite incidental to the main issue: a German postal order counterfoil value 23.50 marks and a letter from Terrillon to a Miss Margaret Coke of Flat 37, 32 Onslow Gardens, which, after discussing other matters, says he is giving the £2 she sent to him to a Mr. Dushan Dokić.

Finally, there is another letter from Dokić himself, and although it is clear that the family are not yet in their new home, it is an apt conclusion to a file which contains so many typical elements in the life of a refugee.

'The particular effort you have made on behalf of my family [writes Dokić to Terrillon] has given me great hope for life and courage for further struggles on behalf of my family. I thank you. We can't send our children to England because they all cling so much to us. Today I received the 23.50 D.M. from you. I can't tell you what this present meant to me, for I must confess quite honestly that when the postman came with it I had nothing but five marks left in my pocket. Believe me, my dear sir, I never cease to repeat: there is a God!'

The original Australian mission seem to have made a mistake when they wrote Dushan Dokić off as a Communist.

III

The Ministerial Director of the German Federal Republic's Ministry for Refugees and Expellees, Herr Werner Middelmann, might have been Curt Jurgens' father in a film. In a building in which, like most administrative buildings in

the Federal Republic, the breath of life seemed the smell of
rubberized flooring, steel, and cement, his office had an old-
fashioned, comfortable atmosphere of mahogany and books.
He had most courteously set aside the whole of an afternoon
to talk to me, and was quick to put me at ease when I
arrived a quarter of an hour late for our appointment. I
explained that I had somehow gone first to the Ministry of
Finance. He put down the copy of the *New York Times*
he had been reading and came towards me, lithe for lateish
middle age, in his light grey suit.

'Mr. Kee, I don't expect it did you much good going there.
Ministries of Finance are less inclined to give than to
receive. It is the same with your Treasury, I dare say. . . .'
We laughed.

Herr Middelmann had first begun to work with refugees
after the end of the war in 1945, but not on the same refugee
problem as that which had concerned Terrillon.

In 1945, as so often in history, one crime against innocent
millions was requited by another. The Potsdam Agreement
signed by the victors in August 1945 arranged for the transfer
to Germany of all ethnic Germans (*Volksdeutsche*) living
in east and south-east Europe, together with the entire
German population of East Prussia and Silesia. These
latter territories were ceded to Poland in compensation for
Polish territories which continued to be ruled by Russia in
the east. A similar mass transfer of population was arranged
from the Sudeten areas of Czechoslovakia.

It was specifically stipulated in the Potsdam Agreement
that these transfers were to be effected in a humane manner.
They were not. Families were uprooted literally overnight
from homes where their ancestors had lived for centuries.
They were packed into overcrowded box-cars which had
little or no sanitation, allowed to take nothing but hand
luggage, and sent off on a four- or five-day journey into
Germany. Many of them, particularly old people and
babies, arrived dead.

The German Government Federal Press Office, whose
political advantage it is, admittedly, to make the most of
these figures, reckons that altogether some 14,500,000

Germans were expelled in this manner, 4,900,000 of them former *Volksdeutsche* and 9,600,000 former German citizens of East Prussia and Silesia. Of these, 3,500,000 went first into the Soviet Zone, though most of them have since left it again to come further west.

It is reckoned that altogether 2,500,000 people died in the whole process.

It is pointless to say that the Germans had themselves inflicted far more terrible suffering on even more people or, what is also true, that the vast majority of the Germans on whom this suffering was now inflicted had tacitly approved of such things being done to other people in the days when to be a good German was to be a good Nazi. Both mass deportations were crimes against humanity perpetrated for selfish political interests. The only possible mitigation of the crime against the expelled Germans is that it was one more of indifference rather than calculation, as the Nazis' crimes had been. Also, if you believe that vengeance plays some part in justice, then this was, like a move in some gigantic national vendetta, crude justice.

For the Germans, left to deal with the expellees almost entirely by themselves at a time when they had almost no resources, there was no sense in complaining, nor indeed anyone to complain to. There was simply a refugee problem to be got on with. 'In those days,' said Herr Middelmann, 'my problem began where the box-cars stopped and the living and the sick and dying were dumped at our feet.'

'And how did you solve it?'

'One moment, please.' From a light grey sleeve emerged a paternal hand which must have carved its way with courteous clarity through the intricate problems of a thousand board meetings.

'All this is only one part of our German problem—the expellees. But on top of these we have another group, the refugees proper, the 3,000,000 or so who have fled from the Soviet Zone since 1948. They come every month in numbers that vary with the state of tension in the world or in the East Zone, but for ten years they were never less than 20,000. There was a slight falling off this year until May, but in that

month there were again 20,000. Altogether, then, counting
both expellees and refugees, there are now roughly
13,000,000 'national' refugees in Germany altogether.
That is to say, one in four of our population are refugees.
For instance, of the 400 people working in my ministry
260 are refugees. My secretary, who you saw, is a refugee—
from East Prussia. . . .'

This attractive, well-dressed young girl hadn't looked
much like my idea of a refugee.

'How far would you say this German trouble of yours is
solved now?' I asked.

'Mr. Kee, if you would say to me, "Is the German refugee
problem explosive?"—and he made the word explosive
sound terrifyingly so—'I would say to you: "No! Most
certainly not!" If on the other hand you would say to me,
"Is the German problem solved?", then I would answer
also: "No." '

So great is the prosperity of the present West German
economy, so apparently limitless its capacity to absorb new
labour that the German national refugee problem is today
mainly a housing problem. During the war Germany lost
a quarter of all her housing. In the densely populated areas
this figure was, of course, very much higher. In Rhineland-
Westphalia, for instance, even including the agricultural
areas, 48 per cent. of the total housing was destroyed.
Altogether, as a result of the devastation of the war, West
Germany needed 2,500,000 new homes.

Herr Middelmann rolled off the figures with unobtrusive
facility. It was as if he had in his head one of those little
machines with handles by which cashiers work out how
much you should get for your travellers' cheques. It was a
pleasure to watch.

'Now then: 2,500,000 new homes wanted for the existing
population. Then: additional population of 13,000,000
requiring about 4,000,000 new homes. Thus: about 6,500,000
new homes wanted altogether. We have built, since 1948,
5,500,000 of these. So you see we have a backlog of 1,000,000
to which must be added, say, another 500,000 to cover housing which has become obsolete and requires replacement.

We are short then at the moment of 1,500,000 homes.'

Sometimes on those little machines in the banks there is a deceptive moment when you think that the total result has been achieved. Then with the gentlest of wrist movements the handle suddenly starts to revolve again. So it was now.

'Now in camps at the moment (well over a thousand of them) we have about 300,000 German nationals, 95 per cent. of whom have jobs and are thus integrated into the economy but who need homes. Normally, 300,000 people would require only 75,000 homes. So you may well ask how the difference between 75,000 and the 1,500,000 that I say we need is made up.'

I asked.

'Because though we have transferred a great proportion of the refugees and expellees from camps to houses it would be incorrect to say that we have fully re-housed them. There is considerable overcrowding in this new housing which must be eased off. What we have done is to transfer camp overcrowdedness behind new walls. These new walls are made of stone and—what is most important—have much better hygienic conditions. This transfer, of course, has a most important psychological effect in addition to the material improvement. But no dreaming, please! It is not pleasant living in new homes with sometimes four or five people to a room!'

'At the present rate of influx, then, when do you think you'll have things as you want them?'

'At the present rate of influx—and the present rate of progress!—we should have built our 1,500,000 new houses in about three years. Though of course we must always remember that we can never be quite sure about the rate of influx of the refugees from the D.D.R.[1] Events in the world, or over there, can have a marked influence on the numbers coming here. And if it did rise considerably then it would make problems for us.'

I couldn't help feeling that some of the more intractable

[1] *Deutsche Demokratische Republik* (German Democratic Republic)—the name of the East German Government.

world refugee problems, such as those of Pakistan and Korea and Hong Kong should be handed over to Herr Middelmann. He made it all sound so clean and neat and soluble as if it really was just a matter of all those figures.

How, exactly, then, had it all been done? How had this enormous housing programme been so successfully achieved? Meticulously Herr Middelmann went back again to the forties explaining how it had then been decided to '. . . try and equalize the burden of the war we lost together.' The 'equalization of burdens law'[2] decreed that all owners of property—estates, businesses, houses, shops—on 20 June 1948 should be charged a sum of up to 50 per cent. of the assessed value of that property on that date (which was that of the German currency reform). Property owners were granted thirty years in which to pay off this sum on which of course interest was charged. This measure has provided two-thirds of the finance required for the building and subsidization of refugee housing. The other third is provided annually by the tax-payer out of the annual Federal budget.

It wasn't until much later that I began to wonder why some sort of similar 'equalization of burdens' principle couldn't be worked out between governments on a world scale for world refugees. An 'equalization of burdens tax' on the property of all individual citizens assessed at some fixed date should not be impossible to arrange by agreement between non-Communist governments. Nothing like 50 per cent. would be necessary, for the proportion of world refugees to the world population is far smaller than that of refugees to non-refugees in the West German population. Probably about 5 per cent. would be enough, although it is in the nature of certain refugee problems—such as those of Hong Kong and Pakistan—that others besides refugees would need to benefit from it. At this moment, however, it never occurred to me to apply the lesson of the German problem to the world at large. Anyway, it would have seemed almost heresy to do so, for Herr Middelmann was proudly making such a specifically German thing of it.

[2] *Lastenausgleichsgesetz.*

First of all there was the thoroughness with which it had all been done.

'You might ask, Mr. Kee, how we were able to assess the value of property of millions of people who had come from territories to which we no longer had access. Well, the equalization of burdens law did in fact involve the recreation of 8,000,000 individual cases. Of course, there were often duplicate files available in this part of Germany, but in the main we had to recreate the various cases, checking and cross-checking on the information received by the individuals.'

'Wasn't it terribly easy for people to tell lies and undervalue the property they'd left behind.'

'No. You see, there, the very number of refugees was a help. You see, though someone may have, let us say, "forgotten" some aspect of business life, his bank manager was probably here too as a refugee and so was his neighbour and his priest. With careful cross-checking it was possible to get pretty near the truth. We reckon that we were able to get within 3 to 5 per cent. of it altogether.'

Secondly, there was the very German philosophy behind it all.

'If anyone asks me *really* how we did it I would say: "by not concentrating on the welfare approach." '

I realized that to Herr Middelmann 'welfare' was almost a dirty word.

'We here in Germany believe in the principle of individual enterprise. The State's only responsibility is to see that each man has the opportunity to exercise his enterprise freely. We saw to this partly, as I have said, by the Equalization of Burdens law for housing, and partly by a very important system of giving help to refugees by unsecured loans. On the principle of encouraging private enterprise we founded the Bank for the Equalization of Burdens. This bank offers unsecured credits to refugees who wish to build up businesses and through it we have already issued credit of some £500,000,000—all, I say, virtually unsecured.'

'Wasn't that rather rash in orthodox banking terms?'

'That was what several of my banker friends in the established banks said. And that was why we had to establish a special bank for the purpose. But I can tell you, Mr. Kee, that our losses on these loans have been only in the range of 1·9 per cent., whereas the average loss for *any* loan business of this type is reckoned as 1·6 per cent. In other words, our losses were only 0·3 per cent. higher than average. I think you'll agree that this is quite an impressive tribute to private enterprise all round. Why— some of the richest men in Germany today have been refugees and built up their businesses from this bank. Take Weiss, the Frankfurt jeweller, for instance, that man was a "hard-core" case in 1950.'

In the pause in which I desperately searched my admiration for some spoke to thrust into Herr Middelmann's meticulously turning wheels, he continued:

'The Equalization of Burdens Bank is, of course, just as much at the disposal of the new refugee as of the expellee of ten years ago. With these new people too, our whole object is to re-individualise the amorphous group of unprotected peoples.'

The phrase acquired a certain philosophical sanctity as he spoke it.

Suddenly, I remembered the widely held view that, in fact, the refugee flood had actually worked to West Germany's advantage by providing her both with a tremendous labour force and a vast internal market. And then, too, there was Marshall Aid.

'Well, now, really Mr. Kee,' said Herr Middelmann who had obviously become very expert at answering this argument: 'If what you say were the case there would be no better solution to *any* nation's economic problems than to invite in a flood of surplus population. If this argument were true I would say to your country in its economic difficulties: "Why, it is all quite simple. All you have to do is to get the population of Australia to return to the mother country!" No, really this is utterly untrue. One is quite wrong in saying that the German economic recovery is due to the refugees. What we have had to put into the

subsidization of refugees and expellees since the end of the war
is seven times what we have got out of them. As for Marshall
Aid—now, we don't for one moment underrate what this
did for us. It was invaluable in getting us a start. But I
would say it was the way in which we used it that was all-
important. We did not just spend it on welfare. To us the
welfare approach without the economic approach means
nothing. In fact, if I could tease my British friends——'
he paused. I tried to convey that I was one of his British
friends . . . 'if I could tease my British friends, I would say
that what happened was that we didn't spend *our* Marshall
Aid on welfare. What you spent on the National Health
Service, we spent on putting people into houses near
factories where they could work . . .'

In all this Herr Middelmann had so far said nothing
about foreign refugees. After all, one might ask, what about
bearing some of the burden which the German's loss of the
war had put on these ex-slave labourers of theirs? Though
it should be remembered that not only did some of these
refugees welcome the chance given them by capture or
deportation to fight against their old rulers, but all of them
were at least given by the Nazi tyranny the opportunity to
escape the Communist one.

In fact, the Germans do bear this burden, technically,
in exactly the same way as they bear that of their own
refugees. The camps containing refugees under the U.N.
High Commissioner's mandate are, as Sophie Lennox
had told me, the direct responsibility of the *Land* governments, and thus indirectly of the Federal Government.
Foreign refugees are entitled to the same social benefits as
any German citizen. New housing for the foreign refugee
is subsidized by the German taxpayer in the same way as
it is for the German refugee. The German Government
matching contributions to the High Commissioner's housing
projects are in the nature of about three to one. Herr Middelmann, with tactful restraint, did suggest that sometimes
such a heavy contribution from the German taxpayer might
strike one as unfair. But there was nothing that could
reasonably be resented as a complaint about this remark.

Indeed, it is questionable how far one would be entitled to resent a complaint. After all, the injustice done to these refugees was often done twenty years ago before some of the taxpayers now paying for their upkeep were born, and before millions of them had had any responsibility.

Theoretically, it was clear that the German record with their foreign refugees was a good one. How far this theoretical equality of treatment was borne out in practice was something I hoped to discover later. In the offices of people like Herr Middelmann it seems almost blasphemy to think that there could possibly be any difference between theory and practice.

IV

The man who first took me into the reality of the refugee world was a youngish, undramatic-looking Englishman with a tired, rubbery face named Watson. If one had seen him at the seaside in an open-necked shirt, one would have thought he was some hard-working, fairly successful salesman like a hundred thousand others. He had been a salesman, but not like the others. Fifteen months ago he had thrown up his sales job and for less than half the salary he had been earning had come out to Munich to work for Françoise Rigby's British Adoption Committee for Displaced Persons.

Watson works with two secretaries at the top of an unimposing building in the Augustenstrasse. His two bare offices have a refreshingly temporary air about them after the more permanent-seeming establishments of the High Commissioner. I was later to be told by a large refugee 'voluntary agency' in Germany that the effectiveness of the British Adoption Committee was greater than that of any other organization working for refugees, including the High Commissioner's office.

'We're not really a voluntary agency proper ourselves,' explained Watson. 'We work through other voluntary agencies. A bit like the High Commissioner's office in a

minor way. Though we're more operational than them
because we do have a few of our own field-workers checking
on what the agencies tell us. You see, what happens is this:
the voluntary agencies bring the cases to us and ask our
help for a refugee—to get a flat or some furniture or whatever it is—and then we look into it and if we have the funds
available we give the go-ahead. We've settled some 2,000
refugees altogether during World Refugee Year.'

'How many unsettled refugees do you reckon there are
still round here—I don't mean in official camps, but in the
unofficial camps and counting the so-called free-livers?'

Something passed over Watson's face which in a less-
unassuming man would have been a flicker of impatience.

'Oh, figures! There are too many figures in this business.
Anyway, figures don't mean much.'

'But the High Commissioner's Office have put out figures
about the numbers of unsettled refugees outside camps.'

'Oh, I know. But I don't see what they can mean really.
In this area round Munich, they haven't made any registration yet,[1] so how can they possibly know how many there are?
. . . Of course, I came out here as a complete greenhorn in
this business and somehow I thought the High Commissioner's office would be useful in giving me information and
that sort of thing. But I found the only way to set about it
was to go out and get it for myself. We simply found as many
unofficial camps as we could and registered as many refugees
as we could. But I'm still finding new ones. Why, only the
other day the chap from the Muslim agency here took me
out to some really shocking places about twenty kilometres
from here. Albanians mainly. There were "houses" there
with notices up saying: "Do not enter. Danger of death.
Building on point of collapse"—and families had been
living in them for nearly ten years!'

The 'unofficial' camp at Schleissheimerstrasse 360 in
Munich itself to which Watson now took me did not, at first
sight, look startlingly shocking. The forlorn brown wooden
barracks lay in a sort of basic symmetry on the flat ground.
Long ago when the temporary huts had been first put up

[1] This was in July 1960.

someone had prescribed a regulation amount of space between them. The few people moving about seemed to have a normal purpose in their movement: a woman walking down between two huts with a shopping basket, a man with a hat and a briefcase, two youths in jeans carrying a large rubber ball. Only the large block of bright modern flats with balconies towering above the place from behind suggested that the people who lived in these huts were in some way second-class citizens.

A crumbling notice, 'Danger! Rat Poison!' had been stuck on the wooden wall of a hut. We knocked at a door. Its opening shook the whole wall. The two rooms had trailing plants and a bird-cage and mats trimly arranged on the crumbling linoleum. The cheap furniture and beds were crowded so thickly round the walls that the floor seemed a precious place. The neatness and cleanliness of the rooms made it difficult to remember that their tenant's one wish was to get out of them as soon as possible.

She was the German-born wife of a Don Cossack refugee and rather a favourite of Watson's. She ' . . . had had a terrible time, poor woman, this last winter—there were times when I wondered how on earth she was going to get through it.' Her husband had been ill and unable to work. She had had to look after her two children of ten and six as well as him. Then she had had a baby, which had died. Then her husband had died. Altogether with her assistance from the German social welfare she had 185 marks per month for the three (about £15. 10s. 0d.), but 14 marks of that (about £1. 5s. 0d.) went on rent for the rooms.

Sitting there now, smiling politely through her spectacles, she might have been a fairly contented housewife anywhere in the world.

'One *has* to be contented,' she said. 'One has to be reasonable.'

Of course, she said, the thinness of the walls was one of the worst things in camps. If it wasn't somebody's radio blaring all day just as if it were in your own room, it was quarrelling and drunkenness and other things that children shouldn't hear. Her little boy, whose blond hair was cut very short, was in bed playing with some red and white counters. Her ten-year-old daughter Eva, a pretty dark girl, sat on the edge of the bed listening to us eagerly, enjoying the first stages of her ability to share something of the adult world. It was an ordinary enough family to all outward appearances.

But to have been a refugee over a long period of years is to have built up an inner world of feeling and experience of which the outsider can often have little idea. For years refugees have been at the same time both part of a normally functioning society and yet not of it. Talking to them, one should tread as warily as if walking through a minefield. A question of mine now produced a sad though almost invisible effect.

With a complete lack of embarrassment, the Cossack's widow explained that Eva was not in fact her husband's daughter. The child was born before she was married, before she ever met him.

At once something happened to the childish eagerness on Eva's face. She went very red, but continued to face towards us as if still sharing the conversation. A few minutes later I saw that she was absorbed in the game of counters which her brother was playing on his bed.

In a few days the two children would be going to Windsor Great Park for a holiday in England. Within a few months they would have moved out of this camp altogether to a new apartment which Watson had found for them. They would be 'resettled'. They were not in any way a dramatic refugee family. Eva, for instance, child of a German father and a German mother, was a refugee only by adoption. Yet she had spent all the life she could remember between these walls through which, and within which, one heard so many things one didn't want to. In one way she had probably been as happy as a healthy child will be in any environment. She would probably cherish for years her memory of the holiday in Windsor Great Park. Yet I couldn't help wondering if the wince with which she had cut herself off from our conversation, and probably many other similar overheard conversations, would not be resettled with her

as a wince against her whole childhood spent as a refugee.
In the next hut Mr. and Mrs. Kryutchik welcomed us
with something like ceremony to the one room in which
they had lived for five years. With an inborn dignity, they
managed to dissociate both themselves and us from this
room as they proceeded vehemently to run it down. The
walls were rotten; the wet and the cold came in; it was
horrible to have to cook and eat and wash and sleep all in
one room for five years. They said all this factually, cheerfully almost, not whining, yet temperamentally different
with their emphasis from people, like Eva's mother, who
say philosophically: 'One has to be contented.'

Mr. Kryutchik was a Ukrainian, brought to Germany as
a prisoner nearly twenty years before. He had been a
carpenter by trade, but was now too ill with stomach
trouble to work. Swiftly he pulled up his shirt to reveal a
long scar from an operation. He was in his fifties, and the
good looks that had once been his now stalked the lined,
shrunken skin of his honest face like a ghost. His hair was
still jet black.

He sat there confirming the description given by his
wife, a youngish German woman, very blonde, in an orange
sweater, of the difficulties of getting by on 110 marks (about
£9. 10s. 0d.) a month assistance money with a rent of
8.50 (about 15s.). Fortunately, Watson had been able to
get them some financial help. Mr. Kryutchik got up suddenly
and started to search among his papers. He handed me a
letter explaining that he had been 'adopted' by the Warfield
Women's Institute. Watson said that this had been arranged
through the same Mrs. Atkinson of the Berkshire Branch
of the British Adoption Committee whose name I had
found in the file of Dushan Dokić.

Mr. Kryutchik said that years ago he had hoped to emigrate. In fact, he had been accepted by the United States
in 1948 and had been all ready to go. Then had come this
stomach illness and he had been rejected. Of course he
didn't want to emigrate now. He had married a German
wife. He knew the language well. He was at home here.
He didn't think much about the Ukraine any more—except

that . . . For one moment I got a glimpse of the spirit which
the United States had rejected twelve years before. Except
that he knew that if he were in bed here dying and heard that
the Russians were at the gates of Munich, he would find the
strength to go out and kill at least ten of them before he
died. And he rose shakily from his chair as he said this and
shot some of them down then and there before us in the
room.

After we had left, I asked Watson if two people could
possibly get by on 110 marks a month in Germany today.

'What?' he said. 'And buy clothes too?'

It was suddenly a great relief to know that someone
professionally in the refugee business was still capable
of feeling angry. The next moment he had resumed his
placid English ordinariness.

'Is there any chance of those Kryutchiks getting away
from that room in the near future?' I asked.

'None at all, I'm afraid, for the moment,' he replied. It
was as if alternative accommodation were simply not in
stock.

He took me into the central corridor of another barracks.
There were some lavatories just inside the front door. They
smelt so foul that I found myself breathing as little as
possible as we hurried past. Glancing in rapidly through the
open doorways, I saw that the walls were peeling and panes
of glass were broken in the lavatory doors.

'Who exactly do these people pay rent to?' I asked.

'The municipality.'

'But I thought you said this was an unofficial camp?'

'That's right.'

'What really is the difference between an official camp
and an unofficial one then?'

'Well, an unofficial camp doesn't have any camp administration, for one thing. And . . . well, it's not written down
on anyone's list as an official camp, I suppose. . . .'

He pushed open a door. A nervous woman in her late
fifties on the verge of tears came towards him, pointing at
one of the two beds in the room. A boy of about thirteen
lay under a patchwork knitted blanket. His face was very

pale. I remembered what Sophie Lennox had said about refugees resenting the number of visitors who had gone round in World Refugee Year staring at them as if they had been animals in a zoo. But, with the same sort of natural courtesy which the Kryutchiks had shown, the nervous woman now tried to stifle her distress and asked me to sit down, insisting that we were not disturbing her. Only when I had sat down did she pay attention to Watson, who was trying to reassure her about her son. Probably just a touch of 'flu; there was a lot of summer 'flu about in Munich this year.

She was a Slovak and her name was Mrs. Golubiev. When she heard that I was from England, she pointed to the patchwork blanket on the boy's bed. That had come from England too, she said. I asked her if she ever got clothes from England.

'Oh, yes.' She plucked at the red-and-white striped shirt she was wearing. It was suddenly unmistakably recognizable as of English middle-class origin. 'I couldn't possibly afford to buy clothes.'

Looking round that sad dim room in which the orderliness and the potted plants evidenced so much determination to make life in it other than sad and dim, and looking at the anxious woman who did this in spite of the stove in the corner and the wash-basin to one side of it and the overflowing rubbish-bucket underneath, I thought of the women in some British Women's Institute or the children in some British school who had spent their spare time knitting that blanket. And I thought too of the English middle-class lady who one afternoon had decided that she must look out some clothes for refugees and had found that red-and-white striped shirt and a few other things she decided she could do without and who, in spite of the inevitable interruptions of an English middle-class afternoon, had managed in the end to find the string and the brown paper and had sent them off. These small things—which the donors at the time possibly doubted would ever reach a worthwhile destination—had probably made all the difference in giving this woman the strength to keep her human dignity.

After we had left we talked about emigration. Watson said:

'It's true that the migration criteria are still slowing things down very badly, but you know emigration isn't really the most important thing any more. What is really wanted now is enough money for integration here in Germany; that's to say, to set these people up in decent housing where all but the small rent they can afford can be covered for them. Most of these people have been here so long now, have got so used to Germany and to speaking German that it's best for them to integrate if they can. I mean, what's the point of any of these people we've been seeing this morning emigrating?'

He paused.

'Though I want to take you now to a family who *are* emigrating. We've been able to fix it up through Lord someone or other—in Kent, I think it is. He's standing as sponsor and giving them a cottage on his estate. Of course, the man can't work; he's too ill. But it's for the sake of the children really. . . .'

There were five children in the family altogether, all of school age. Three of them, two girls and a boy, were together with their parents in the two small rooms in which they lived, when we called. The children shook hands politely, bowing slightly. Their clean, handsome appearance made an astonishing contrast with their home, which was so small that no housewife could have made it attractive. The kitchen and living-room in which the father had his bed was about the size of a kitchenette in a London flat. The inevitable stove, wash-basin, and open rubbish-pail were jammed into the corner. The pail was full of potato peelings. The other room was a little larger. The three beds were jammed together in it, so that looking in through the door, one wasn't aware of the floor at all—it was like looking into a corner of a sale-room.

The father, a Bulgarian who had been in Germany since the early days of the war, sat on his bed ('I've never seen that man anywhere except sitting on his bed,' said Watson afterwards), and tapped his body, explaining about his illness. His wife, a former slave labourer from Poland, had a handkerchief tied round a swelling on her jaw. The hand-kerchief ended in two rabbits' ears on the top of her head. When she spoke, one saw that most of her front teeth were missing. She said she was worried about whether she would get her false teeth or not before they went to England. She didn't want to arrive in England looking like that. I asked Watson in English if she knew that she could get false teeth on the National Health Service once she got to England. He said 'yes', but she hadn't wanted that—she wanted to start life in her new country looking her best, and had been prepared to try to save the money to buy her false teeth in Germany. The Adoption Committee, he said, had in fact been able to look after that for her, and she would be arriving in England looking her best.

The children proudly brought forward their school reports. One of the girls didn't seem to have done quite so well as the other two, but she seemed just as proud. I found myself staring at them, wondering how children who had been brought up in such a place could look so alive and clean and happy. I remembered a remark of some child refugee quoted in a pamphlet: 'Oh, yes we have a lovely home, but we haven't got a house to put it in.'

'Just think what an asset those children can be to a country,' said Watson afterwards. 'I wish you'd seen the other two as well.'

'But why have they had to wait all this time?'

'Oh, well, this is under the Special United Kingdom World Refugee Year scheme, you see. The father couldn't possibly have passed the normal immigration criteria in his state of health. And a family like that would never have split up. But the criteria are relaxed under this new scheme.'

'But if those children are going to be assets to us now—which they certainly are—surely they would have been assets years ago and could have been spared having to live in that dreadful place all this time?'

It was, of course, pretty silly to say this to a man like Watson, but I badly felt I wanted to say it to someone.

'Oh, I quite agree with you,' he said.

We came out through the sour, sweaty smell of the corridor into the sunlight. The camp site was a nondescript enough sort of place, but to be under the open sky was for a moment a wonderful experience. Behind us the coloured balconies of the block of flats behind the camp shone bright and gay.

I asked Watson how much a two-roomed flat in a block like that would cost.

'Oh, that's a private builder. For Germans, of course. About 400 marks [£35] a month, I should say.'

'And what could a refugee who was working afford to pay?'

'Oh, around 75–100 marks. Though sometimes, if you pay a lump sum down at the beginning of a lease, you can get a flat like those ones over there for that sort of rent. But then you've got to find the lump sum first—say about £300–£400. And, of course, you've got to find a German landlord who's prepared to take a foreign refugee from a camp. Though that's another matter.'

As we left the camp, I looked back once more at the flashing balconies above the dead, damp huts. Something, I thought, seemed to have gone wrong with Herr Middelmann's principle of the Equalization of Burdens.

We visited two more unofficial camps that morning.

'Actually,' said Watson as we arrived at the first one, a collection of stone barracks. 'This one's not even officially an unofficial camp.'

'You mean it's official, then?'

'Well, no; not that either. You see, when the High Commissioner came down here in connexion with the out-of-camp programme recently, one of his people showed him this as an example of an unofficial camp. Personally, I can't think why they didn't show him the one we've just seen in the Schleissheimerstrasse. Anyway, he saw this and said it wasn't bad enough. So as a result it's fallen between two stools. It doesn't qualify for the out-of-camp programme nor, because it's not an official camp, does it qualify for camp clearance.'

'What is it, then?'

' "Integrated in the German economy" I suppose it's called.'

The Pumycz family, Ukrainians, had been living here for nine years. There were now eleven of them altogether and they lived in three rooms and slept in five beds. Maria, the fourteen-year-old daughter who was at home looking after the baby while everyone else was out, was the only member of the family to have a bed to herself. She had lived her whole life in huts, she said. Though the outside walls of this one were of stone, the inside walls were wooden, and as thin as those in any other camp barrack block. She showed me where these walls were peeling and where they were damp and where the rain came through in winter. 'In winter everything's *so wet*,' she said in violent protest, though she had never known anything better.

Maria's father, Dmytro Pumycz, worked as a labourer and earned 370 marks (about £30) a month. His children's allowances brought this up to 650 marks (about £54) a month. Watson had once told me how, when he first started working in Germany he had had about 600 marks a month for himself and his wife and his two children, and had found it difficult for the four of them to get by on that. Dmytro Pumycz had nine children. I told Maria that I was from England, and she showed me a knitted patchwork blanket on one of the beds. 'My father would very much like to go to England,' she said. 'We all would.' But he had been rejected for some reason even under the latest World Refugee Year scheme.

Watson told me that there were a number of middle-class intellectuals in this camp. Life, he said, was often particularly difficult for such people because, although there was an almost limitless labour market for manual workers in Germany, it was not always easy for an ageing intellectual to find a job. We called on a cheerful, intelligent-looking Ukrainian woman, Mrs. Polenska. She was living in two very neat, clean rooms which were crammed with furniture, but in which a standard of *bourgeois* respectability was upheld. Cushions stitched with Ukrainian embroidery were arranged tastefully about the large divan bed. Her

'. . . I noticed that there was after all something a little different about it' (see page 40)

Mr. and Mrs. Romaniszin

'Every year for ten years we have tried. This year we have not bothered. . . .'

husband was away in Munich, where he had just managed to find an office job. Before the war he had owned a chemical factory in the Polish-administered Ukraine. They had been deported by the Germans in 1944, and had spent the last sixteen years of their life together in camps, the last eight of them in this one. I noticed that Mrs. Polenska, unlike the High Commissioner, did not think of herself as living in anything but a camp.

'Even after all this time,' she said, 'what I mind most is the terrible drunkenness and the other awful scenes we have to witness.'

She had been tying up a very large parcel as we came in, and she explained that she was sending unwanted clothes of hers off to relatives in Poland. 'One must do what one can for people who are worse off than ourselves. Now that my husband has work in this office, things are all right for us. But before, when we had no work—well, I can tell you . . . Yes, things were very short . . . it was difficult to manage. Yes, he did try to emigrate ten years ago—to the U.S.A.— and he was rejected as unfit.'

'Oh, well,' she went on, 'that was ten years ago'—as if she felt embarrassed for the United States immigration authorities. She went on doing up the string of her parcel.

As we were leaving, a rougher-looking Ukrainian woman came in to see Mrs. Polenska. I stopped and spoke to her, but though polite, she didn't seem to want to answer questions. Oh, things were all right. Yes, she managed. She said this in a way which conveyed that just now things were not too all right, but she wasn't going to make them seem any worse than they were by admitting the fact to a stranger. She looked anxiously across at Mrs. Polenska and then started to go out again. When Watson and I made it quite clear that we were going, she stayed.

'You know,' said Watson as we walked away to our car, 'That man Polensaka is the son of a priest and he's like a sort of priest in that camp. Almost everyone in the camp goes to him or his wife for advice when they're in trouble of some sort.'

We got into the car.

D

'I think there's just time to show you one more place, but I don't want to be home too late. Actually, it's pretty lonely for my wife here in Germany, and I'm nearly always home late.'

We drove off.

'I don't want to stop and talk at this place, if you don't mind. There's a man there who's more or less off his head and who keeps pestering me. He's a sort of priest too—as a matter of fact I don't really know if he's a real priest or not. I just know he's a terrific nuisance. . . .'

After a time I saw that we were driving along the side of a desolate piece of land, no bleaker or more interesting at first sight than the nondescript waste you find in the left-over areas of any big city. Then I noticed that there was, after all, something a little different about it. The back-ends of old motor-buses which lay scattered among the weeds, and the collections of corrugated iron and boarding which else-where might have been just dumped scrap or at best places for housing neglected allotment tools, here housed human beings. Washing hung on lines between some of the piles of scrap like festoons of giant convolvulus. Some of the back ends of buses sprouted crazy chimney stacks. Small children scuttled like rats among the rubbish.

'This is the place,' said Watson a little nervously.

He drew the car up in the shadow of a big new building on the other side of the road. I opened my camera.

'Perhaps you might be able to photograph it through the window of the car,' he said hopefully.

In the end we both got out.

Once we were on the other side of the road, the weed was in places high enough to act as some sort of natural cover. I watched some children climbing up the steps of the patched and stranded charabanc that was their home, and I couldn't help thinking that if I were a child I would rather live here than in one of the more orthodox unofficial camps we had seen that morning. There was certainly more individu-ality in the architecture here. There was more open space too. An adventurous prairie wind stirred in the weeds and the rusty iron.

Somewhere in the middle of this desert a shack sprouted wooden crosses instead of chimney-pots. I stared at it fascinated. The next moment it was too late.

A wild, bearded figure in a long cassock strode round the front of what I realized was a pathetically makeshift church.

'Look out,' hissed Watson.

I clicked my camera, trusting to the distance to make me inconspicuous. With an ostrich hunch of the shoulders, I turned and walked away.

A shout challenged us across the stunted wilderness. Watson made discreetly for the road like a boy caught stealing apples. Once I too had reached the road, I allowed myself a quick look back. The self-appointed spiritual guardian of this waste land was shaking his fist at me, scattering his words wildly on the wind.

Who was he? How had he come here? What rites went on in that tumbledown travesty of a church of his?

As we drove off, Watson told me what he knew of the place. About twenty families lived there altogether, mostly German refugees—two or three foreign refugee families, he thought. Probably a proportion of 'a-socials' there—people who *wouldn't* live anywhere else rather than couldn't.

'Though I suppose,' said Watson, and I wished there had been some refugee 'experts' there to hear him, 'you couldn't exactly write the small children off as a-socials.'

'What do they do for sanitation there?'

He shrugged his shoulders.

'And water?'

'I expect there's a tap around somewhere.'

When we got back to his office, his secretary had put a file on his desk with a pencilled note attached to the front of it. For the first time that day I saw a really disturbed expression cross Watson's face.

'Oh dear,' he said quietly.

His secretary came in and said: 'It's all right. They say he's out of danger.'

Watson handed the file and the note across the desk to me.

'This is a single man whom we eventually succeeded in

getting into a flat and finding a furniture grant for. After a great deal of trouble, we'd just got him properly installed, and now—well, you'll see there—he's been found by a neighbour lying unconscious on the floor of his flat with gas poisoning.'

Watson's job was to live in the refugee world as if he were part of it—to deal with each problem as it came along. It is a world much like the greater one it overlaps, in that few problems are ever finally soluble and that the best you can ever hope for is to be able to take whatever comes next in your stride. The only difference is that in the refugee world there is even less room and time in which to manœuvre.

'Accidental, I expect,' said Watson. 'And, anyway, as you heard, the hospital says he's out of danger. . . . By the way . . .'

'Yes?'

'I don't know whether you'd be interested, but next week I'm going off on a tour with a man from the Muslim agency to see some of the out-of-camp cases he wants to draw my attention to. I could probably arrange for you to come along too, if you like.

'I'd like to very much.'

We agreed to make the final arrangements later by telephone.

'Right. Well, see you then. I must get back home to the wife now. I'm afraid this isn't much of a life for her.'

V

The largest concentration of official camps in Germany is in the Stuttgart area. Sophie Lennox had made a point of breaking her week-end to come down from Bonn and take me round.

Before setting out we had to confer with the High Commissioner's Stuttgart representative, a young-middle-aged

Norwegian named Jan Høst. Høst was the sort of man who combines an air of urgent anxiety with one of competent self-assurance, so that just when you are beginning to think that there's a little too much of one, you are caught unawares by the other. Thus very effectively he undermined the twin charges of smugness and incompetence to which any international civil servant automatically tends to find himself exposed.

It was quite untrue, he said, that the High Commissioner's office had no proper record of the out-of-camp and unofficial camp refugees—in his area at least; he couldn't, of course, vouch for any of the others. But he could guarantee—yes, guarantee—a 100 per cent. full register which they had compiled from the lists of the various voluntary agencies. (Munich, added Sophie Lennox, had admittedly been a bit of a problem lately.) Nor was it true that the High Commissioner's staff couldn't really know much about the practical side of the refugee world just because they were not operational. It was true, said Høst, that they were *technically* non-operational. However, the High Commissioner's office did pay the salaries of some twenty-three counsellors for the voluntary agencies and thus, through them, had their fingers on the pulse.

When talking to members of the High Commissioner's staff, one is constantly finding oneself up against two apparently irreconcilable sets of facts. The first is their own overwhelming conviction that they are doing a first-class job in the only way in which it can possibly be done in the circumstances. The other is that a great many refugees who want decent houses are still in camps after many years and that a great many more who for many years have wanted to emigrate are still unable to do so. In order to preserve sanity, it becomes necessary to demolish one or other of these two sets of facts.

Why was it, I protested to Høst, that the re-housing had been such an interminably slow business? After all, the disgrace wasn't just that adults had been kept refugees all these years, but that children were being turned into refugees retrospectively.

Høst, who, like any member of the High Commissioner's staff, could pass a written examination in humane, liberal thinking with flying colours, quite agreed that this was terrible, but insisted that things were going ahead as fast as he and his colleagues could possibly make them. After all, the Germans had 13,000,000 odd refugees of their own.

I asked if he didn't think that, after what had been done to the foreign-speaking refugees during the war, they didn't have some moral right to priority in the society which had treated them as slaves. This, said Høst, was a point of view.

I think if he had been answering the question in that examination paper he might have said that he shared this point of view, but again like all members of the High Commissioner's staff, he was a good diplomat. The Germans, he reminded me, give the foreign-speaking refugee complete equality with their own refugees. I must remember too that in any housing project arranged between the German authorities and the U.N.H.C.R. the Germans bear about three-quarters of the cost.

But did this nominal equality of treatment always work out in practice? Wherever I travelled in Germany, I saw huge new blocks of apartment houses being put up for German refugees. Surely, in all this activity it could have been possible to find accommodation for the 25,000 odd refugees Terrillon had given as still 'unsettled'? It was said to be rare now for a German refugee to have to wait more than six months in a camp without getting some sort of housing. Of course, as Middelmann had pointed out, many of these Germans were housed in temporarily overcrowded conditions. But if given the opportunity of overcrowded conditions in decent housing and overcrowding in the sort of camp I had already seen, I couldn't doubt that any refugee family would choose the former. Of course, too, there was the perfectly reasonable point that it was only natural for the Germans to give preference to their own people, and that foreign refugees were an international responsibility foisted off on to them by an international agency in 1951. But, though reasonable, this was not the official line. And the High Commissioner's representatives were in Germany partly to see that the official line of equal treatment was adhered to.

It seemed probable that any prejudice which might be operating against foreign refugees would not be at governmental level. Watson, in Munich, had said to me: 'It's all very well saying that the foreign refugee is treated equally with Germans. On paper he is. But some of the petty officials simply treat them like dirt.'

I asked Høst whether local politics were a factor that counted against the foreign refugee. After all, in the allocation of land for building it was the local politician who had the say. And local politicians live by votes. Foreign refugees didn't have votes, though German refugees did. Perhaps it was asking too much human nature to expect that the foreign refugees should get equal treatment where the allotment of land for building was concerned.

Here again Høst's qualities as a diplomat were predominant. A lot of his work, he said, consisted indeed of negotiating with local mayors and such people about the allocation of land for housing projects. He found them agreeable people.

After that it seemed best to start seeing for myself again.

I had so often seen official camps distinguished from unofficial ones on paper that I had somehow expected them to look different. I suppose I had even thought that they would look better. My first sight of the official camp at Unterjettingen brought me back to reality.

The approach was pleasant enough. We left the highway and drove up a winding road through cornfields. It would have been pleasanter, though, if we hadn't known that we were going to a camp at the end of it. This knowledge made it a lonely road. Soon we were driving into a darkening pinewood. A fine rain started to come down, and with it a sense of isolation and gloom.

Barbed-wire, all strength and purpose long since rusted from it, appeared strung along posts among the trees. We turned in through a gap on to the site of an old Wehrmacht ammunition dump.

A number of different sorts of hutches lay rotting in the rain on the floor of the wood. Some were lavatories, some wood-sheds; some held rabbits and others people.

There was a welcoming shout. An everyday life of a sort was going on here. A woman who recognized Høst called out that she had a letter in Norwegian about her three children who were on holiday in Norway, and she wanted him to translate it for her. We went up some steps into her room.

Soon I was to find it difficult to react spontaneously when shown with dignity round these innumerable sad, almost identical little rooms, with their cheap furniture stubbornly trying to assert some pride in the crowded space, and the flowers and trailing plants striking a sudden, sophisticated note. Now curiosity was still alive. Ignorance prompted questions. It was still possible to be taken by surprise by the flowers.

Mrs. Rosa Kerekes, a Hungarian, had three rooms, in one of which was a stove. All were clean and neat. But there was the same smell that I had noticed in the Schleissheimer-strasse in Munich—a smell of old cooking and sweaty clothes which had long ago saturated damp wood and re-emerged in its own right. Her husband was dead, but she just kept going with her social welfare money. She had help from England sometimes too. Yes, a Women's Institute had sent her that patchwork blanket over there. The worst thing about this barrack was that the washroom was so far off— away at the other end of the camp. Yes, the taps down there were the only ones in the camp. She had been in these rooms eight years now. It was too long. But she was glad for the children about this Norwegian summer holiday that had been arranged for them. Høst began to translate the letter and I wandered away alone to other parts of the camp.

A small, dark, youngish man, an Albanian, was standing in his doorway as if he had a world to survey. He lived in the little, dark room behind him into which he invited me. He was married, but he didn't live with his wife. She was no good. She slept with other men. I asked if he knew where his wife was now. Oh, yes; she had a room in the next hut.

There was another bed in the room which was much
dirtier and dingier than any of Mrs. Kerekes's. In fact, there
were no sheets on either bed—only limp, dark blankets.
And wrapped up in them on this other bed was a fair-haired
man of about the same age as the Albanian. There was
something limp about him too. A small, rather strained
smile on his face. There was a broken tooth in the front
of his mouth. I asked the Albanian if the man were ill.
'Oh, no.'

He said it as if no further explanation was required. I
repeated the question to the man on the bed. But he simply
went on smiling. The broken tooth made the smile seem
shifty, and, as if the man had suddenly become aware of
this himself, it faltered. He said nothing.

'He doesn't speak much German. He's a Ukrainian,'
said the Albanian.

I asked the man on the bed if he were all right. The smile
came back again, but as a sort of shrug.

'Do you get enough to eat here?'

The broken-toothed shrug was repeated. It was as if he
had understood the sense of the question, but not the point.

'He doesn't understand much about eating,' said the
Albanian. 'He's not very interested in it.'

I spoke directly to the Ukrainian again.

'Do you have any money?'

'Fifty.'

He had answered at once, as if all the time he had been
able to understand everything I was saying.

'Fifty marks?'

'A month.'

The words just seemed able to trickle through the gap
between the broken tooth and his slightly curled upper lip.

'You can't buy much with that,' said the Albanian. His
smile seemed quite a lively thing by contrast with the rest
of what went on in that place.

Suddenly, I realized two dreadful things. First, that there
was in fact nothing wrong with the Ukrainian in these
greasy blankets except that both his body and his mind were
indistinguishably overwhelmed by the most terrible inertia.

How many years already could he have lain there like that? How many more years would he lie there?

The second realization was in a way even more dreadful. It was that the Albanian had no particularly companionable feelings about his companion in this dismal shed. He was showing him to me in the same sort of way in which he might have shown me where the roof leaked or where a rat had eaten away a floor-board.

As if to try to deny the reality to myself, I said to the man on the bed: 'Would you like to emigrate?'

An answer came back: 'Don't know.'

Again a faltering checked the smile round the broken tooth. And yet it was just in this moment, when the whole ability of the man to move at all seemed to make a mockery of human personality, that I thought I saw in his eyes a perfectly normal, almost a sharp expression. It was as if there were some sort of signal there, a flicker of a suggestion that if only it could receive some recognition it could use some help.

'It's all right,' said Høst when I got outside again. 'We'll be moving him to a mental home in a few days time.'

'Oh, good,' I said weakly, but I knew quite well that this was not the sort of help the man had signalled for.

The next man to invite me in to his room was a strong, hearty-looking Yugoslav of forty-eight. Oh, yes, he was quite contented here. There were strips of linoleum on his floor and a clock on the wall. He switched on a radio. Also on the wall were the blue, white, and red horizontal bands of the old Royal flag of Yugoslavia, and beside it a picture of Mihailovic. Comfortable music surged from the radio, and a fatuous pair of voices, a young man's and a young woman's, crooned that all was well with the mid-morning world. The rain dripping through the trees outside made the music seem cosier still. This man had lost his wife; his four children were in a children's home. He could earn enough money to buy himself the things he wanted by working on building sites. Yes, all in all, he liked it here.

If you had met this man anywhere in the world you would have recognized in him a sensible, reliable fellow, sound still in wind and limb, a little individualistic, perhaps, but free of those tiresome neuroses which make a man rebel unduly against such environment as comes his way. The sort of man, in fact, who makes society what it is. And yet as I walked out again into the rain, into the faint smell of garbage and sanitation dampened by the breath of rotting wood, this man seemed in his way as ill as the inert Ukrainian.

A few doors further down a little, black-haired hunch-back woman was watching us with the bright eyes of a mouse from her dripping doorway. She made no obvious effort to catch our attention, but the moment I spoke to her she invited us in, as if she had planned it like this from the start. A crucifix and a crutch hung on the wall. She showed us a photograph of three children; a girl aged ten and two boys of eight and five.

There was only one bed in the room, and I asked her if the children lived with her here. No; they were in children's homes. They were in children's homes, she repeated. She looked at me appealingly, thinking perhaps that I was some official with my note-book. And, oh, they were so miserable.

How did she know. Did they write?

No, but two months ago she had been to see them there. She had spent three days at the home and had seen their little faces, so thin and pale with crying. They were wretched and unhealthy, and they didn't get enough to eat. Quite suddenly, as she turned to Høst, her small twisted frame began to shake. Bright tears started rolling from the black eyes in her tiny, handsome face. Her grief was all the more distressing for its miniature proportions. She wanted the children back here, in her little room, she said. Even though it was overcrowded she would manage all right. The children were so unhappy without her. Why couldn't they come back here? Even if it was unhealthy for them here, it would be better for them, just because they would be with her. They had never looked so ill as when she had seen them at the children's home.

Høst comforted her and said that he was hoping there might be a possibility of getting her a flat near one of the

homes. But he couldn't promise anything. Her recent
agitation made her look very fragile as we left.

Were these children's homes really as bad as she made
out, I asked Høst.

'All orphanages are *per se* bad institutions,' he said
sensibly. 'But these are decent and well-run.'

He looked for the first time as if the alliance between his
self-assurance and his anxiety were not always an easy one.

'Would you like to know the truth of that woman's
story?' he asked.

'You mean it wasn't true what she said?'

'Well, in fact, her three children were taken away from
her because she didn't look after them properly. She doesn't
have a husband. The children are all by different men. Her
way of life in this camp made her neglect them terribly.
It was clearly much better for them in the circumstances to
be in a children's home, though I think it would be a good
idea if we could get her into a flat nearby.'

Somewhere with this truth the other truth had to be
reconciled: the truth of the tears welling from the black
eyes, of the agony that was the agony of any mother for
her children.

But Høst was giving me the breakdown of the camp
figures. There were 152 refugees here altogether, of whom
104 were under the mandate. The distinction seemed more
than ever absurd. I was still thinking of the little hunch-
back. The main trouble with the people here seemed
suddenly to be not that they were refugees (within or
without the mandate), but that they were human beings.
Pessimistically I inspected the three taps and the trough
that served the 152 human beings for washing facilities.
Wet slops and garbage spilled foully from the brick refuse-
containers as we made our way back to the car.

'Who then exactly is the official responsible for the state
of this official camp?' I asked Høst.

'It's the local municipality's responsibility,' he said, and
added: 'I must certainly speak to them about that refuse.'
He must have sensed what I was feeling. 'Of course, this is
the worst camp in my area,' he said.

'But, as diplomatic representative of the refugees in Germany, couldn't the High Commissioner make the hell of a fuss about the way in which a camp like this is kept?'

'It's not our policy to improve camps, but to clear them.'

'But as they seem to be taking so long to clear, couldn't you do *something* to make them more tolerable?'

'Oh, yes. Well, of course, the High Commissioner has the right to make his voice heard. The Germans run the camps, but we're the watchdogs.'

'Couldn't you bark a bit more then? I mean, couldn't you, for instance, personally, kick up a row about the state of Unterjettingen?'

'I could to a certain extent. But I'd have to clear it with Terrillon first.'

As we drove away we passed a dilapidated hut displaying the sign *Gaststätte*. Crates of empty, upturned beer bottles lay outside, abandoned in the rain.

On the way to the next camp Høst stopped in the small town of Sindelfingen.

'I want to show you a camp in the final stage of clearance,' he said.

We drove into a side lane towards a factory chimney. The Mercedes sign, like the symbol of some religion, proclaimed what went on there. A number of executive's cars lay arranged on the asphalt of a newly made car-park. On the edge of the car park broken concrete stumps lay beside some newly ploughed-up earth. Høst looked surprised. He spoke to bystanders.

'Oh,' he said, turning to me. 'The last of the barracks was cleared on 1 July. There were three of them last time I was here—standing on this bit of land that's all ploughed up. The car park's been built on what was once the rest of the camp. I expect they'll be expanding it further now.'

I stared, impressed by this unmistakable progress.

But on the other side of the road were three familiar ex-Hitler wooden-type barracks.

'Those aren't refugees,' said Høst quickly. 'They're

foreign workers, Italians mainly, imported to work in the Mercedes factory.'

We went and looked at one of the big new apartment blocks into which people from the Sindelfingen camp had moved. This had been built by a High Commissioner's project in collaboration with the German Government. Here there was nothing to sour the sense of progress. It was a fine, airy structure on a small prominence, still smelling of new concrete. Each apartment had its own little bright blue balcony. Mrs. Kura, a tall, middle-aged Polish woman with her hair tied up in a turban in the manner of an office-cleaner, showed us round her airy three-room flat with kitchen and bath. Her five children followed us round as if for them too it was still something special to look at. Until Mrs. Kura had moved in here a few weeks ago she had been living in camps for seventeen years.

She brought out her rent bill to show me how the 103.70 marks a month she paid for the flat was made up.

'What's this for *Schönheitsreparaturen?*' asked Høst suddenly. 'You shouldn't be paying that. I'll have to look into it.'

He made a note.

'And then there's this for water, too,' said Mrs. Kura.

Høst went over the bill again. 'No; that's all right. But it's this 6 marks for decorative repairs I'm not happy about.' He made another note.

As we walked down the steep slope away from the building to our car he said:

'It's very important to keep in touch with them properly after they've been put into decent housing. This thing is, of course, quite trivial—possibly some mistake. But it's important for them to know we're still there to help them. Too many people make the mistake of thinking that housing is synonymous with complete integration. After seventeen years, you can't expect anyone to feel integrated overnight.'

About twenty minutes later, driving ahead, Høst waved an arm from his window at the official camp of Malmsheim. It lay on a ridge commanding a fine view of the Bavarian

countryside. Up there in an old Luftwaffe camp to enjoy it
were 335 refugees altogether, 236 were German and 99
foreign ex-D.P.s.

The German camp administrator took us round. His
attitude was that of a warden in a benevolent almshouse.
It was a camp that was in slow—very slow—process of
being cleared. Formerly it had held a total of nearly 800.
Since 1959 no more refugees had been admitted. There was
a leisurely, spacious atmosphere about the place. Some of
the wooden barracks were now quite empty. Although there
was the same smell here of latrines and garbage and damp
wood that has been lived in by too many human beings, there
was not the same feeling, as at Unterjettingen, that human
beings had here reached the end of the road.

But Mrs. Szalik had been here for nine years and in
Germany for eighteen, ever since as a very young girl the
Germans had carried her off from her home at Lwow.
She must have looked then very like her fourteen-year-old
daughter, who was sitting alone doing some home-work as
we came into the hut.

The girl answered questions shyly. Of course, she said,
the whole family wanted to emigrate. She said it as if it
were something that was not really within reason for her to
wish for, like winning a football pool. Yes, they had tried
to, but it had never come to anything. She didn't remember
the details. We'd have to ask her mother when she came in—
she was about somewhere. Her father was at work. Where
would she herself prefer to emigrate to? Her eyes shone for
the first time. Oh, Belgium. Why Belgium? She once spent
a holiday there.

Outwardly Belgium cannot have seemed so very different
from Germany. But I realized that for her it had been the
one country where she didn't live in a camp and that therefore it was automatically the most wonderful country in
the world. There for the only time in her life she had felt
herself part of something other than the refugee world.

Her mother came in, a dumpy, cheerful little woman.
Like every refugee housewife I spoke to in these camps, she
immediately turned our visit into a graceful ceremony,

making us sit down in her best chairs. The room was about 18 ft. × 15 ft. altogether. A cardboard partition divided it in two. There were Coca-Cola advertisements on the wall; roses in pots and fuchsias in buckets. An electric iron sat under a bed.

Yes, she said, she and her husband wanted to emigrate. To Canada. Yes, she knew her daughter wanted to go to Belgium, but she thought she'd be happy enough in Canada when they got there. She talked as if the family actually expected to go soon, and I asked her if this was so. Well, not exactly. But once before, many years ago, they had applied to go to Canada and had been rejected. Why? She didn't really know, but she had applied again under some new scheme and hoped that it would come off this time. She was such a congenitally cheerful person that she almost managed to make it sound as if she could take another rejection and another stretch of years in camps in Germany in her stride.

I asked her if she would like to emigrate to any other country, if for some reason it should not be possible to go to Canada. No, she said, only Canada, and her eyes shone in the same way as her daughter's eyes had shone when she said so definitely 'Belgium.'

'Canada!' she said, as if it were somehow hers, as other people talk of football and cricket teams they support.

What about England, I asked? England was taking more people now. Would she like to come to England if she could?

For a few seconds I could see politeness struggling with outspoken honesty. She let out a gay laugh, looking at me all the time and trying to judge whether or not I would take offence at what she was going to say.

'Ah, England! No. Anywhere but England. In England too much fog!'

I tried to persuade her that this wasn't really true, that England was not wrapped in fog *all* the time. She listened politely, prepared to change her mind if she could be properly convinced.

Was there really no fog in England in the winter?

Eugene Danchenko

Alexander Terlecki

Head Doctor of Sanatorium

'You can't leave people lying about. Something happens to them.'

Bill McCoy

'It all requires a bit of fenangling, you know.'

Well, of course, sometimes there was some fog, but to suggest that there was fog all the time . . .

Her laugh rang out again. 'Ah, no! In England, fog! For me, Canada!'

And then suddenly very seriously she explained that though on the whole her eighteen years in camps had left her in good health, her lungs were sometimes bad in winter, particularly when it was damp, which was why she so much wanted to emigrate, because it was so damp in these wooden barracks. But there would be no point, would there, in emigrating to a damp, foggy place like England? I didn't try to argue with her. She had set her heart on Canada, and who was I, anyway, to raise her hopes about England, even if she could have been persuaded to want to go there? There were enough people in England, I knew, to sponsor all the refugees who wanted to go there, but would the Home Office, even under the new World Refugee schemes, let them in? World Refugee Year hadn't helped the Pumycz family in the Moosacherstrasse, Munich, very much.

I left this cheerful Polish housewife with her hope of Canada.

Afterwards I found out why she had been rejected for Canada the first time. She had been what, in the jargon, is described as 'socially handicapped'. That's to say, she had not been married to her husband, although she had two children. Now that she was respectably married, she was hoping that there would be no difficulty. What she didn't know was that the present Canadian scheme was for refugees who had been previously rejected because they were physically unfit. And though she had enough trouble with her lungs for the damp to bother her, she wasn't technically unfit. Anyway, even if she had been, she had not previously been rejected for that reason, so she could not be eligible for the new scheme. Her chances of being accepted this time were almost nil.

After this Polish room with its roses and its fuchsias, the one in which Mr. and Mrs. Romaniszin, two elderly Ukrainians, were living in another barrack, seemed sadly dingy. But they too welcomed us with gracious hospitality.

There weren't enough chairs to go round, so they sat side by side together on the bed.

For ten years now the Romaniszins had been waiting among the cupboards spilling untidily with worn-out clothes and the gay elaborate pictures of straw and painted wood that Mr. Romaniszin had made, hoping all this time to be allowed to join their daughter, who had emigrated ten years before to the U.S.A. She was married now and living prosperously in Philadelphia. The reason her parents had not been able to join her was that a photograph of Mr. Romaniszin's lungs showed signs of earlier tuberculosis.

It was impossible not to reflect that if for ten years in this foul place he had managed to remain healthy and active enough to execute the elaborate pictures now on the walls behind him, then in all probability he would have been that much more active and productive in the healthier atmosphere of the United States. The last ten years had plainly aged an already ageing man, but he still had the spirit to show a bewildered dissatisfaction for, all his patience, and the energy to convey his and his wife's intense desire to see their daughter again.

'Every year for ten years we have tried. Every year we have sent new photographs of the lungs. Every year we are deferred again. This year we have not bothered to send the photograph because they told us there might be a relaxation.'

He didn't sound as if he had much faith in anyone else's optimism now. But only death would make him give up hope altogether.

VI

'The dignity of the human spirit' is a phrase easily come by in a civilization like ours, which pays more and more lip-service to it as it respects it less and less. Anyone in search of the reality behind the slogan in the nineteen-sixties could do worse than visit a refugee camp, for here, in the sense of an innate capacity to triumph in utter loneliness, if necessary, over the most crushing circumstances of defeat, the human spirit's dignity is found in all its simplicity. Mr. Romaniszin's achievement for civilization is as great as that of the loudest-trumpeted statesman or field marshal. One visits the refugee world expecting to sympathize, pity, and help, and one goes away, not only shamed out of all patronage, but inspired by example for the whole business of living.

The official camp of Neckargartach lies in a clay-pit on the outskirts of Heilbronn. The cliff of the pit skirts the cluster of wooden barracks with a dramatic skyline, so that down there at the bottom among the hollyhocks in the little gardens you could imagine yourself, if you turned your back to the main road and half closed your eyes, to be living simply in a rather stark and exciting landscape. Only when a horse and cart, which should be tiny, lumbers gross and contemptuous round the outline of the pit does reality assume its true proportions, and you remember how from up there it looks as if a cluster of maggots were eating their way into the hillside.

In one of these huts lives Mrs. Szrednicki, a Polish woman, with her fifteen-year-old son Ludwig and her seventy-eight-year-old mother, Maria Koslowska. On the afternoon on which I saw them, Mrs. Szrednicki's other child was also there and her twenty-one-year-old daughter Julia, on a visit to her old home from Munich, where she had been in lodgings for a few months, studying for a medical scholarship. The father had died several years before and Mrs. Szrednicki was out at her job as a book-keeper in the nearby Fiat factory. Ludwig, Julia, and Maria Koslowska were sitting together in the long wooden room, which, except for two elaborately constructed models—one of the Eiffel Tower and the other of the Bridge over the River Kwai—was like hundreds of others in European refugee camps.

There was in fact nothing to show that I was in the presence of remarkable people except perhaps Mrs. Koslowska's appearance, which, with her hair only just beginning to turn grey and her eyes brisk and alert behind her spectacles, was that of a woman a good deal younger than seventy-eight. She herself had been a refugee twice in her life. She was an Italian by birth and had married a Pole who was later declared 'missing' in the civil war after the Russian Revolution of 1917. As an Italian, she had been allowed to leave Russia by the Soviets and had travelled on an English ship via Odessa to Italy, whence she had gone back to the new independent state of Poland in the hope of finding her husband. She had lived near Warsaw for the next twenty-four years. Her daughter had married a Polish industrialist. Then, after the Rising in 1944, the Germans had deported the entire family. Julia had therefore lived in camps since the age of five. Ludwig had been born in one. They had had their home here in this clay-pit in Neckargartach since 1952.

Talking to the three of them—to Maria Koslowska in French because she refused to speak German, though she knew it well, to Julia in the English which she had learnt perfectly, though she had never been to England, and to Ludwig in German, in which, like Julia, he was bilingual—there was no indication whatever that these people's lives were in any way different from those of other members of the intelligent European bourgeoisie whom one might meet anywhere in the world. Yet Ludwig had spent his entire life in refugee camps, and Julia too could remember nothing else.

It occurred to me that with these two particularly intelligent and articulate young people there was a chance to find out what it was really like to be a child in a refugee camp. One could put to them the sort of questions which one couldn't in fact put to a child. For a child's mind has no wish to formulate abstract views of a situation which involves itself. I said to Julia:

'As a child in these places, were you aware that there was anything specially unpleasant or different about them? Or, since you didn't know anything else, do you really think you enjoyed life here just as much as you would have done anywhere?'

Her round, open face looked very serious beneath the

bell of black hair. She stared straight in front of her. At first I thought it was as if she were in communication with the refugee child that was still part of her, relaying my question and trying to interpret its answer in adult terms. Then, as she still didn't answer, I thought that my question had been too clumsy, and I was thinking about how to rephrase it when she spoke:

'I hated the camps,' she said. 'I simply hated them. I hated the overcrowding and having to get up in the morning with so many other people in the room. And I hated the drunkenness and the fighting going on all round us.'

I asked her if she thought that her personality had been affected by the experience.

'No. Because I had a good mother and a good father.'

Later she said: '. . . I was ten years old when I decided to become a doctor. I had a friend whose father was a surgeon, and he used to tell me about his work. This was in Coburg Camp—it was not a bad camp. This friend's father worked in a hospital and we visited him there. I liked it all so much when I saw it because it was so clean and orderly—not a bit like the camps. And after that, when we played the sort of games that children do, I was always the doctor. Then here in this camp we had a very nice children's doctor—a refugee. He was so nice to us children. I decided I would like to be a children's doctor.'

She was about to take a scholarship exam. for Heidelberg. If she won it, it would give her enough money to keep herself there for the six and a half years necessary to qualify as a paediatrician. If she didn't win the scholarship . . . 'Then I shall have to think of something else.'

But it was obvious that she couldn't really think of anything else yet. And for me too the possibility that the force for good, which life had transmitted to her so strongly and so simply in these foul places, should be wasted for the lack of a relatively small sum of money seemed also too terrible to contemplate.

'Of course,' she said, 'both I and my brother are about three years behind in our studies because we had to learn German before we could learn anything else in the school.

But that has been the only handicap in being a refugee.'

Ludwig also had no doubt about what he wanted to be. His answers were short, polite, and forceful.

'Atomic physicist,' he replied.

'Where? Here in Germany?'

'Oh, no. I shall emigrate.'

'Where to?'

'That's simple. U.S.A. or Canada. I shall finish my schooling here. Then wait until my sister has finished her studies. Then go.'

'What do you find you need most that you haven't got in the camp?'

'Knowledge.'

He had built the Eiffel Tower and the Bridge over the River Kwai as a hobby in the evenings. But what he wanted was books to study, and they cost money.

'With knowledge,' he said, 'you can do anything.'

One hears much current talk today about scientific break-throughs and new frontiers, but somehow I have never felt so closely in touch with a new age as talking then to this sixteen-year-old boy in a dilapidated hut at the bottom of a European clay-pit.

It was getting late, and I went out in search of Sophie Lennox. We had another camp to visit that day. I found her near the gate, listening to an excited-looking one-legged man with a crutch. He held a letter in his hand.

He too was a Pole, named Waluga. Before the war he had lived and worked in France. He had come to Germany during the war and had married a Polish girl, who had borne him five children. These children, like the Szrednickis, had spent their whole lives in camps.

A few weeks ago Sophie Lennox had brought a French journalist to Neckargartach. He had been interested in Mr. Waluga as having a French 'angle', and had written about him in his article which appeared in an illustrated magazine. Now as a result of this article Waluga had received a letter from a workers' organization in Lyons. It guaranteed him a job and temporary accommodation in a three-roomed apartment, with the promise of five rooms later on. Showing

Sophie Lennox the letter he had the same almost frightening expression of tense excitement on his face that revolutionaries have in the first moment of serious triumph.

As we drove to the next camp, I couldn't help wondering about the individual stroke of chance which had liberated Mr. Waluga and his family quite suddenly from the refugee world after all this time. Was it possible that the official bureaucratic machinery which for one reason or another had been unable to liquidate his and thousands of other similar problems over so many years had indeed developed a sterility from which the refugee needed to be liberated as much as from the camp? Now that there were relatively so few refugees, might not individual enterprise on behalf of individual refugees, cutting through the red tape in which each case now seemed so inextricably entangled, be the best way to attempt a solution?

We drove several kilometres to the parade ground of wooden huts that was the official camp at Bad Cannstast. The parade ground was lined with depressingly permanent-looking streets and gardens. It occurred to me that for all the words I had seen written about the 'steady progress of camp clearance' there had in fact been remarkably little sign of it in the camps I had been shown so far. Of course, I knew that the figures had been going down slowly, but only at Malmsheim, where the Romaniszins and the Polish housewife who feared the fog lived, had empty rooms caught my attention. I asked Sophie Lennox how many people there were here in Bad Cannstast.

'Three hundred and nineteen, the last time I was here,' she said. 'But I expect it will have gone down since then.'

We went to the camp administration. I asked how many refugees there were in the camp.

'Three hundred and twenty-one.'

I looked at Sophie Lennox.

'Ah, you mustn't be too depressed by that,' she explained plausibly. 'You see, naturally, as camp clearance progresses and certain camps become emptier, we move out any small numbers who may be left so that we can clear the place completely. Then we move these into other camps. In other words, it's quite possible to have the population of one individual camp actually go up temporarily in the case of camp clearance.'

I asked the camp administration if this was what happened at Bad Cannstast.

'Well, no, actually. It's just that there's been a baby and one person has come out of prison.'

The special feature of Bad Cannstast is a vast junk heap of old motor-car chassis which forms a skyline to the flat camp just as the lip of the clay-pit does at Neckargartach. Perhaps it is the pointed symbolism of this mountain of rejected machinery beside which human beings have been dumped as if they too were of no more use that gives to Bad Cannstast its particular air of bitterness.

Alexander Terlecki was brought to Germany from the Ukraine as a slave labourer at the age of eighteen in 1942. He has been living in camps ever since, and in Bad Cannstast since 1950. He is married and has two daughters—Maria aged thirteen, and Stephan-Roma, eleven. I picked him out at random in one of the camp streets. He had a lean, intelligent boyish face, and it seemed to me that if one had met him in the streets of any European or American city one would have taken him utterly for granted in that normal background, though one might have noticed in passing the particular openness of his expression. What aberration of national, international, or charitable bureaucracy could have condemned such a man to bring up his family in this dreadful place? Stranger still, how had he been able to resist so successfully its demoralizing imprint?

The first thing that struck me in talking to him was that it no longer occurred to him that he had any real chance of ever getting out of the place. And this seemed a terrible thing at the end of World Refugee Year. Yes, he had heard of that, but. . . . He shrugged his shoulders. A shadow of bitterness moved across his face as if such fine-sounding things were not for him. Oh yes, he said, he had tried to emigrate, years ago. But it seemed hopeless. Why? Was he ill? No; he was perfectly fit. He could work at anything, however strenuous. He had a job as plate-layer at the moment.

Was there something the matter with his wife, then, or his children? No; they were all perfectly fit. He said this with a slight look of resentment on his face, as if he couldn't quite see the relevance of my question. But why then had he been unable to emigrate? Oh, well, he had tried to get to America in 1950, but in 1948 he had spent six months in prison for a black-market offence, and this had disqualified him.

There had been a period, I knew, around 1948 when the Americans had imposed severe sentences for comparatively trivial offences in a determined effort to stamp out the black market. Whether in equity it could truly be reckoned as a criminal offence for a young man who had spent three years in Germany as a slave to continue to fend for himself at the end of that period in the only way he had learnt, is arguable. What is not arguable is that it is unjust for a man's punishment to continue after he has served his sentence. For that was exactly what had happened. Terlecki had been virtually sentenced to ten years in Bad Cannstast, as well as to his six months in prison. And his innocent wife and unborn children had been sentenced with him.

He had made another attempt later to emigrate to Canada, but had somehow got the impression that if he had been accepted he would have had to pay his own passage, so he had given up the idea. He couldn't possibly have raised the money. I asked Sophie Lennox how he could have got this idea, and she confirmed my impression that in fact the Intergovernmental Committee for European Migration would have paid his passage. She couldn't think how he had got the other impression. I put this to him, but it was clear that the whole incident had long ago got lost in remote confusion in his mind.

'Well, that was what the agency told me.'

Was it? Or had he misunderstood? And if he had understood, why had he been allowed to drift on indefinitely so helplessly in this misunderstanding?

Here in fact before me was an example of the vast gap that existed between the reality of the European refugee situation and the situation on paper. This man was perfectly healthy. He had a nominal 'social' black mark against his name, but it was of a sort which countries had in recent years increasingly come to regard as insignificant. In World Refugee Year, in which there had been supposed to be special consideration for such cases, it should not have been very difficult to have him moved. And yet not only was he still here in the same camp to which he had been condemned ten years before, but he was completely in the dark about his chances of getting away from it, and, what was worse, fatalistically accepting the dark. For him—and for how many others like him?—World Refugee Year simply might not have existed. Theoretically, I.C.E.M. his agency, the High Commissioner—all were there to help him, but somehow he had sunk without trace between all three of them.

I asked him if he still wanted to emigrate. The sun was sinking and shone a soft, subtle light on his face. For a moment it illuminated an expression which otherwise would have been instantaneously eclipsed by the swift cloud of bitterness which followed it—a momentary expression that was almost imperceptible and yet one of indescribable agony.

'Of course I want to emigrate,' he then said. 'I don't want to live here among the Germans. We are nothing in all this.' He waved an arm around to signify the society which lay beyond the dumped cars. 'Have you seen all the housing they are building? All for Germans. It is a German world here. We work for them as we did in the war, but otherwise they have no use for us. We cannot settle here.'

'Would you go to England if you could?'

'Yes, of course.'

I thought of those 500-odd still untaken sponsorships. I thought of the house that I had heard of which an Urban District Council in England had donated for a refugee months ago but for which it had been unable to find a refugee.

'Did you apply to the recent British Commission that came over?'

The old look of fatalism came over his face. He hadn't heard anything about that. And, anyway, these commissions came over here, sat miles away somewhere; you had to pay your fare there, lose a day's work, and then you were rejected at the end of it. What was the point? How many people had that happened to! But in fact he hadn't heard anything about this latest British one.

I turned to Sophie Lennox.

'But don't the migration commissions come round all the camps, then?'

'Oh, no. You couldn't expect that. They wouldn't have the time. It would be quite impossible.'

I had a sudden mental picture of intelligent men in clean suits trying to be as broad-minded as possible.

'No, they sit at a number of central points and the refugees come before them. But this man's voluntary agency should have let him know about this one.'

I asked Terlecki how often he saw a counsellor from the voluntary agency. 'Oh she comes once or sometimes twice a week perhaps.'

'You mean there's only one?'

'Yes, I think so.'

Later, when talking about the atmosphere at Bad Cannstast, he said almost ashamedly: 'I'm afraid the atmosphere's not at all good in this place.'

'Why do you think that is?'

He looked bewildered for a moment, as if it hadn't occurred to him that you could really pin down a reason. Almost, it seemed, because he could find no other reason, he said:

'Well, for one thing, the counsellor here isn't really any good.'

It didn't seem to occur to him that what he was really saying was that the one link between individuals like himself and the vast network of international, national, and organizational bureaucracy which had theoretically been marshalled to help him, was no good. But the really terrible thing was that if he had realized the implication he would probably have accepted it fatalistically.

The sun had now quite gone down. But his face lit up properly once before we left him.

'Would you like to see my hares?' he asked suddenly. His eyes shone quite startlingly bright and eager.

We walked over together towards the skyline of junked

iron. Just below it on the edge of the camp there was a battered contraption of hutches behind some wire netting. Terlecki stepped nimbly inside and picked up some rather placid-looking hares by their long ears. He had twenty of them altogether and twelve does. As he held them up for us his face was as full of the excitement of living as anyone's I had ever seen.

A friend of Terlecki's came up and watched too. He introduced himself as Michael Muzica, thirty-eight, also from the Ukraine, but he had an ugly wound in the throat and it was difficult to understand what he said. Yes; a war wound, when he was taken prisoner in 1941. Yes; in camps ever since. His breath smelt rather strongly of beer, though he was perfectly sober. He seemed to stare at the animals through the wire netting with nostalgia, as if there was something there which he had irrevocably lost.

As we turned back to the main road of the camp to find our car, a tall, very powerfully built man in a red shirt came round the corner of a hut, and shouted in our direction. It was a shout of such foul and bitter frenzy that I thought for a moment he must be shouting at us. He swept a huge-fisted forearm through the air. But he was only summoning his daughter into the hut. She was a good-looking girl of about fifteen, and was walking arm-in-arm with a girl-friend of the same age when the shout came. She looked back and unlocked her arm easily, unhurriedly, as if she had often heard that shout before. But there was no question of her not obeying.

'Of course, you get a good deal of drinking in a camp like this,' said Sophie Lennox understandingly.

VII

'The word "refugee" is inevitably bound up with the denial of the right to live one's life and to work through one's life as one wants to because of arbitrary manifestations of

power, and this goes back into history. What's special to
our times is that for nearly fifty uninterrupted years now—
since the Balkan wars of 1913—such manifestations of power
of one sort or another have been at work. . . . The thing
about the refugee is that he is a man who is besieged by
fear.'

A rather wizened little nut of a man with gold-rimmed
spectacles talked a little unnaturally in a bare room on a
quiet July Sunday afternoon in an empty villa on the outskirts of Salzburg; a thin veneer of 'conference American'
lay over his fine north of England accent. On his desk there
was a silvered crucifix—though he was no clergyman—and
a little mobile plate with his name on, which looked at first
like that of any other executive, but which on closer
inspection revealed that the name, instead of being in brass
on a black metal background, had been woven with meticu-
lous care in straw. It was a present from one of the thousands
of refugees whom Mr. Arthur Foster of the World Council
of Churches had fought for in the course of eleven years in
the Austrian side of the business.

Quietly, without any pretence that it was a pleasure,
but also without any suggestion that I was ruining his
Sunday afternoon, he had agreed to come down to his office
and talk. We had about two and a half hours before my
train left for Germany. Throughout all that time he never
looked at his watch.

The rather formal opening was slightly disappointing.
This was the man of whom I had been told:

'Of course, the High Commissioner's people say thank
heavens there's only one Arthur Foster.'

This was the man about whom one of the High Commissioner's people in Bonn had actually said when I mentioned his name. 'O God!' in a way which made it clear that
they wished they could have felt as contemptuous of him as
they were trying to appear. This was the man who, when he
had heard what had sounded to him like a High Commissioner's edict to get old people into old people's homes,
had risen at a conference and shouted: 'Look here! When
I'm so old and finished that I'm going on my hands and

knees, you can come to me and tell me to go into an old people's home *and I won't go!*'

Arthur Foster had begun to interest himself in refugees as long ago as 1917, when he met Belgian refugees while working as a lay preacher in Cumberland. But in spite of his opening words, his was no specialist, academic interest in the status of the refugee. Throughout the twenties and thirties he had concerned himself with what he called 'our own British refugees'—meaning the unemployed and down-and-outs, the rejects of a harsh social system. What he cared about was human suffering and whether that suffering was technically within anybody's mandate or not doesn't mean a thing to him. Possibly his one limitation is that he cannot properly understand how it can mean anything to anyone. Sitting listening to him, it is difficult not to share this limitation with him.

He talked of the recent British mission bitterly. He'd put up thirty refugees approximately and only one or two had been accepted. But, as I was to realize later, he might have been temporarily forgetting that the British mission was restricted by its terms of reference to refugees who had been in Germany or Austria before January 1955. It was clear certainly that he had little regard for British (or American for that matter) government officials at work in the refugee world. Of the delegates to the High Commissioner's Executive Committee he remarked with a fervour that enabled me to see for the first time the true man behind the careful formal opening: 'Oh, they're usually nice enough fellows in themselves, but as far as refugees are concerned they don't know a bee from a bull's foot.'

His criticism of the High Commissioner's office was forceful, but balanced and rational.

'Look,' he said. 'There's one thing I want you to get straight. I'm all for the principle of the High Commissioner's office, as any sane man must be who has the welfare of refugees at heart. The High Commissioner's office is the one real hope for refugees. First, it ensures for the refugee decent diplomatic recognition and representation of his legal interests. Secondly, it's the one organization through which government moneys can be channelled to refugees. So don't go saying I run down the High Commissioner's office, because I don't. Of course, I have criticisms of it. . . .'

There were, it seemed, two special features of the situation in Austria which I would learn more about when I visited the country later on. These were: (1) the continual flow of refugees from Yugoslavia and (2) the position of certain one-time D.P. foreign refugees who were now Austrian citizens. A lot of the incoming Yugoslavs and all of the recently naturalized foreign refugee Austrian citizens failed to receive consideration as refugees from the United Nations High Commissioner, and this seemed to Foster idiotic. When he explained the mixed causes behind the flow of refugees from Yugoslavia, one saw that this attitude of his was not simply made up of resentment and impatience, but that it was informed by expert knowledge and the deep feeling that comes from knowledge.

'Do you know what *slava* means'?

'No.'

'Well, it means something like the glory or oneness of the family and it's very important in central Europe. Now, in poorish countries like Yugoslavia, when a man dies there's simply not enough of the patrimony to divide up properly among the family and give everyone a living. If you did that, there wouldn't be enough to go round and the family *slava* would be destroyed. So in Yugoslavia, as indeed in other parts of central Europe, there's a tradition that the younger sons emigrate to seek their future in other lands and thus keep the family intact at home. It's been going on for years and years, and the traditional gateway out from Yugoslavia has always been Austria. Well, now Communism has tried to put a stop to this. It wants its young men at home to work for the State. But a people's family traditions are stronger than Communism, so the young men are coming out secretly all the time. Ninety per cent. of the current flow of Yugoslav refugees are single men. Now the Commissioner says these people are simply *economic* refugees, and therefore considers them outside his mandate, but I don't know where the difference is myself. The words of the High Commissioner's mandate talk about "fear of persecution"; well, if it isn't persecution to prevent a man from seeking his future where he wants to seek it and where his family traditions demand he seeks it, then I don't know what is. . . .'

He said that in 1959 about 50 per cent. of all Yugoslav refugees had been refused refugee status and had been forcibly returned to Yugoslavia by the Austrians.

'As for the other 50 per cent. well, you probably know about the various restricting immigration criteria—they hold back the new refugees just as they've done the old. Of course, World Refugee Year has helped to get things eased a bit. I should say now that migration is just about keeping pace with intake here in Austria. As a new refugee you've got a reasonable chance of getting out in six months, and remember that emigration—where possible—is by far the best form of rehabilitation for a refugee. . . . By the way, I wonder what the civilized world would think if Austria at the frontier said to a refugee: "Are you blind, or have you got two legs, or T.B., or whatever it is, because if you have, then you can't come in"? There'd be an outcry—and rightly. But that's exactly what these other countries are doing, only it doesn't look so bad, because they can take advantage of the fact that Austria's given the refugee asylum in the first place. What it amounts to is that they let a poor little country like Austria bear the burden of their own consciences. . . .'

I asked him about the second category of refugee, which he said had been unrecognized by the High Commissioner. These were the former D.P.s and foreign refugees who had become naturalized Austrian citizens.

'The High Commissioner himself was responsible for getting them naturalized. And it was a good enough idea at the time, because a few years ago there were definite disadvantages in not being an Austrian citizen. The Austrian Government generously agreed to the idea. But now, ironically, when so much more is being done for refugees and you've got the camp-clearance scheme and this out-of-camp programme coming up, well, of course, these naturalized refugees are the losers, because they're not eligible as

Austrian citizens. So they have to go on sitting there in these
rotten, filthy, verminous structures that have simply stood
on their rotten posts ten years longer than they were ever
meant to. . . . I was talking the other day to one of the High
Commissioner's people in Vienna about Feffernitz, which is
the largest residual camp in Austria with well over 1,000
people in it, and I was told we have no mandatory refugees
there. . . . The High Commissioner's misleading the public
with his camp-clearance scheme. He won't have the money
nor the personnel to liquidate the *total* camp population in
Austria by the end of 1961. . . .'

I asked about out-of-camp refugees. Did the High
Commissioner's people search these out here.

'Good God, no! We do it for them!'

'What about the statistics he puts out, then, about out-
of-camp refugees?'

'Look here. If he comes to me with those statistics I say
to him: "Your statistics are all cuckoo, because it isn't until
we find a case that you know anything about it!" '

'What's really your main complaint against the High
Commissioner?'

'Now don't get me wrong. I'm not complaining that there
is a High Commissioner. As I said, the refugee would be
lost without him. And the people in his office are all good
guys. I know them and like them personally. But in the
actual *working* of the thing . . . well, one thing is he tends
to make holes and then look for a refugee to fit into them.
We in the World Council look for refugees and then make
a hole to fit them in. He's supposed to be non-operational,
but then he has these programming departments hundreds
of miles away in Geneva and lays down his schemes with no
direct knowledge of refugees in the field and then expects us,
who *do* know, to fit in with them. We don't know whether
he's operational or not. In fact we don't know *what* he's
doing. In fact, I'd say to him: "Give over pretending that
you're not operational and come into the field, and then at
least we'll know where we are. . . ." '

'Well, what's the sort of thing that goes wrong from the
refugee's point of view as a result of this confusion?'

'The High Commissioner receives his money to integrate refugees. Well, you don't integrate refugees by just moving them from A to B. It's no good just putting up housing for them and moving them in and thinking you've done the job, because you haven't. The refugee's been paying, say, 50 schillings [15s.] a month in rent for his camp accommodation. Now he has to pay, say, 400 schillings [£6]. Well, his earnings on the average in Austria will be around 1,400 schillings [£20] a month. With that change in his rent, his budgeting is going to be pretty tight. When you move a man, you've got to take into account his earning capacity, his working capacity and his psychological reaction. Mass housing projects are no good if they're not at economic rents. If the High Commissioner had bought a quarter of the number of houses he *has* bought and provided them at economic rents, at least he'd have solved properly a quarter of the problem that way. . . . Then there's furniture. A flat's no good without furniture. Well, the refugee can probably get that on a loan from the High Commissioner. But it's no good saying to a man: "You can have a flat and a loan to furnish it"—if the whole operation's going to make him so tight for money that he can't begin to repay his loan. We've never asked that the refugee should not stand on his own feet. Nor have we denied that it's all too easy to demoralize a refugee by charity. But we do say that the refugee cannot be expected to compete economically with the Austrian in rent-paying. After all, in Austria, though there's no shortage of jobs at the moment, it's only the lowest paid manual jobs that are available to refugees. And supposing you can't work? Do you realize what the public welfare is in Austria? Two hundred and seventy schillings a month! I defy anyone alive to live on that! What we say is, that camp clearance programmes and all the rest of it are fine, but they must be carried out in accordance with the refugee's ability to pay.'

I said: 'It seems to me that what you'd really like would be for the High Commissioner to provide all legal and diplomatic representation of refugees, to carry out all the negotiations with governments and put on political pressure

behind the scenes for money, to work out programmes in
full consultation with the agencies—really taking the lead
from the agencies—and hand over the money to them.'

Foster smiled so widely that I thought the wise, nut
face, hardened in so much other people's suffering, would
split.

'Something like that,' he said.

'But then in order to get really big governmental funds
don't you want as co-ordinator some overall World Refugee
Organization larger than the present High Commissioner's
office?'

'I don't really like the idea of relying on governmental
funds. The moment you have them, you get the money
used in the sort of way it is in U.S.E.P.[1] I much prefer
the insecurity of private donation. No——' and he suddenly
looked very serious. 'The important thing to get across
to people is that the refugee problem in our time is an on-
going problem. It's not just an emergency problem which
you can deal with by rule-of-thumb methods, or fixed ideas
of one sort or another. Nor can you deal with it by charity
which you simply apply dutifully and look the other way.
We've got to get across the fact that this is an on-going
situation and one that people in the West will have to live
with probably for the rest of their lives. . . .'

As he drove me to the station, a long way out of his way,
he relaxed again.

'Of course, you know,' he said, 'anyone has to be mad to
get into this business . . . and loony to want to get out of it
once he's in.'

⁺VIII

Watson hadn't been at all sure how far we would be going
when we first discussed the trip. He thought the man from
the Muslim agency who was taking us had said Bamberg.

[1] The United States Escapee Programme, see p. 9 and later, p. 88.

But when he looked at the map and saw how far away Bamberg was from Munich he said:

'That's funny. I thought he said we'd be back easily in the day. Perhaps I misheard him.'

His finger roved modestly about the map closer to Munich.

'Ausburg?' he suggested without much conviction.

I don't think he cared how long or how far he drove in search of refugees who needed help. But I think he probably thought quite a lot about his wife who found it lonely in Bavaria without friends and who spoke little German.

When I rang him to make the final arrangements it was Bamberg after all.

'We'll be calling in at one or two quite interesting places on the way,' he said encouragingly, 'but we'll definitely be back within the day.'

We made a date to meet outside the Munich office of Jamat Al' Islam, the Muslim agency, 'as close to seven-thirty as possible.'

The morning train from Stuttgart was due in at Munich at seven-twenty. In the clean clear light I stared from the train at the lush, undulating Bavarian countryside. We passed a signal-box with the word 'Dachau' on it. A few hundred yards further on we passed through a trim, pink station with geraniums hanging from the roof in bowls.

We got into Munich about twenty minutes late. The agency's office wasn't far from the station. I ran along the pavement against the stream of secretaries and citizens with briefcases going to work. A self-effacing, ordinary-looking British tourist with a camera slung round his neck drifted into my path. It was Watson.

'It's all right. We were going to give you another ten minutes.'

He introduced me to a hatless, dark-haired, competent-looking man in thick horn-rimmed spectacles: Ahmed Balagiya, a Yugoslav, once a refugee himself and now head of the Muslim agency. Also, to Mrs. Berghaus, a deeply sensible-looking, middle-aged social worker in thin-rimmed spectacles who was employed as 'counsellor' for the agency. She was born in Russia, but had left in 1928 and had

married a German. She had been working among refugees
for some years now, and in her face tiredness and understanding had combined into a fairly permanent expression
in its own right.

As we drove out through the Munich suburbs towards
the Autobahn we talked of the refugee situation much as
people going to work anywhere at that time might have
been discussing the familiar background to their day. I
told Watson of my general impression of the High Commissioner's office to date. Mr. Balagiya, whose agency had
for a short time been in sharp conflict with the High Commissioner's office, smiled pleasurably. I asked Watson if
he thought that something like the same professional,
bureaucratic disease which appeared to paralyse so much of
the High Commissioner's activity was also to be found
among the agencies.

'Well, I'm sorry to have to say it,' he replied, 'but I think
that often one does have an impression of too many agencies
fighting for a case-load among themselves. Certainly, there's
a good deal of redundant activity. This is partly because it's
easier to get money from the High Commissioner and
U.S.E.P. for projects if you have a big case-load, but, of
course, jobs do undoubtedly come into it too.'

I looked for confirmation of this both to Mr. Balagiya
and Mrs. Berghaus.

They nodded.

'Oh, undoubtedly.'

'After all, a lot of these people in the agencies have had
their jobs now for fifteen years or more. Well, as the problem
tapers off, they ask themselves why they should be the ones
to go. . . .'

Certainly, I thought that the tendency to cling to jobs
would be a more or less unconscious factor, both in the minds
of agency workers and of members of the High Commissioner's office. But it did seem probable that it was there in
both cases. Unconsciously, it would encourage people to
make even heavier weather of the problem than necessary.
Unconsciously, it would discourage them from trying to cut too
drastically through painstaking, settled methods of procedure.

Once we got on to the Autobahn Mr. Balagiya seemed able to dissociate his mind entirely from the business of driving. He told me about his own case-load, which consisted mainly of Muslim Yugoslavs and Albanians, but also contained some unexpected elements. For instance, there were some 3,000 Algerians from France at the moment living and working in Germany. In one sense it was impossible to say that they were refugees, and certainly they were politically too embarrassing for the High Commissioner to have anything to do with them. But these Algerians found it more comfortable to live and work in Germany. In France they were liable either to suspicion from the French authorities or else to pressure from the F.L.N. to undertake anti-French activity.

Then there were some hundreds of so-called Turks in Germany who had started their refugee lives under the protection of the United Nations High Commissioner, but had long since lost it. These were ethnic Turks from Russian Azerbaijan or Turkistan who had been either deported to Germany or captured with the Russian Army during the war. Immediately after the war the Russians had sent a collecting mission round the camps, in the course of which, with Western acquiescence, many thousands of Soviet citizens who would have preferred to become refugees had been forcibly repatriated. In order to escape this fate, these Soviet citizens from Turkistan and Azerbaijan had claimed and been granted Turkish nationality as ethnic Turks. They went to Turkey, became Turkish citizens and received Turkish passports. The economic atmosphere of Turkey, however, was very different from that of Germany's *Wirtschaftswunder*.[1] Hundreds of these former refugees returned to Germany, where at least they could get jobs. Unfortunately, since they now possessed Turkish passports, they could no longer get refugee assistance from either the High Commissioner or the United States Escapee Programme.

From the back of the car Mrs. Berghaus handed me the file on a case of this sort. The man's name was Anver Hazer.

[1] The 'Economic Miracle'.

He was thirty-six years old. With his wife and six children, he now lived in a room in Munich which measured 20 square yards. He had a job as a truck-driver, but the conditions in which he lived were described as being those of 'very grave need'. The family had little furniture, slept on straw mattresses on the floor, and had only just enough money on which to keep going.

Having seen something of refugee conditions myself by this time, I realized suddenly how subtly hardship is falsified by the very fact of being put into an ordered file like this. For it thus automatically acquires some sort of place in the scheme of things, whereas the essence of social hardship for refugees is the indifferent neglect it represents, dulling the soul as the cold floor chills the bones.

Hazer was born near Baku. His family were enrolled on a collective farm when he was five. At seventeen he had gone into the Soviet Army. A year later, in 1941, he was taken prisoner. He hated the Russians; he saw thousands of fellow prisoners starving to death in German prison camps; so he joined the Azerbaijan Legion of the Wehrmacht and fought the Russians until 1945. After the German defeat, he managed to escape the Russian repatriation teams and came into an U.N.R.R.A. camp, where he first became a camp policeman and then took an U.N.R.R.A. training course as a motor mechanic. In 1947 he got a job driving for the municipality of Ganghofen, in Lower Bavaria. There he married a German girl, by whom he had a daughter. In 1949 he was resettled by the I.R.O.[2] in Istanbul and acquired Turkish nationality. He worked there as a taxi-driver until 1953, when his second daughter was born. This second child's health couldn't stand the hot climate. So the family had returned to Bavaria, where Mrs. Hazer's relatives lived.

Again I wondered at the simplicity of a file. How many other conscious and unconscious reasons and half-reasons must have gone into the decision to return? And what did he think of the decision now, living on about 480 marks a month (£40), with his wife and six children and sleeping

[2] International Refugee Organization; see p. 6.

on straw mattresses on a stone floor? I remembered how a few days before Watson had spoken from personal experience of the difficulties of trying to keep a family of four on 600 marks a month.

'You see,' said Balagiya. 'A foreigner like that gets the worst of both worlds. He's automatically handicapped in the labour market by being a foreigner, and he hasn't a hope of being given housing, because he's not a refugee.'

'What on earth can you do about him, then?'

'The only hope is to buy him a small flat with a reasonably low rent, by paying key-money. About 3,000 marks (£250) would usually do it. Of course, we'd probably have to help with the rent even then. As I say, the High Commissioner's people aren't interested in him, because he's not within the mandate.'

We had been racing down the Autobahn for some time now. After a while signposts to Nuremberg began to appear.

'We'll be seeing out-of-camp refugees mostly today,' said Balagiya. 'But there's one of my people I want to call on in the camp at Valka.'

'What did you say?'

'Valka—near Nuremberg.'

I had heard much of this notorious camp. For years it had been the main reception camp for all new refugees entering Germany. Conditions in it had been so bad that it had been constantly cited in Communist broadcast propaganda as an example of the terrible disillusionment that awaited refugees in the West. A nineteen-year-old Czech refugee named Frantik Suchy, who had been received there, had later returned to Czechoslovakia in disgust, and had said over Radio Pilsen:

'I had to leave that awful camp at any price, for the conditions there kill within a man all his good qualities; you face hopelessness, misery, and despair with every step you take.'[3]

Of Valka the Zellerbach Commission sponsored by the International Rescue Committee had written in 1958: 'Nobody defends Valka; nobody wants it; everyone agrees

[3] Quoted by the *Zellerbach Commission Report*, 1958, Section VI, p. 4.

that it is an abomination. . . . But Valka still stands. . . .
In Bonn a high-ranking official concerned with refugees
assured members of the Commission that the Government
was determined to see Valka closed by the end of 1958.
His categorical affirmation is something that will be welcomed by all those, both refugees and agency representatives, who have experienced the horror of Valka at first
hand. The Commission wonders, however, whether some
way could not be found of accelerating the schedule of
closure in the case of Valka. Every day that it continues to
exist is an affront to the conscience of the German people
and, indeed, of the free world.'[4]

That had been written in 1958. In July 1960, just before
I left on my tour of Germany, I had received a document
from Herr Middelman's office stating that there were now
only 164 refugees in Valka and that it was in the process
of closure. All the necessary functions of a refugee centre
were being transferred to the newer camp at Zirndorf. On
arrival in Bonn, I had asked Sophie Lennox if I could see
Valka.

'Valka is now closed,' she had said.

'Are you sure?'

'Oh yes, Valka is closed—thank goodness,' she added
piously.

And now here was Balagiya telling me that he was going
to take me to see one of his refugees in Camp Valka.

'But the High Commissioner's office told me that Valka
was closed!'

He shrugged his shoulders agreeably.

As soon as we left the Autobahn and began driving along
ordinary roads again, the endless blocks of new apartment
houses being built by the Germans on the outskirts of every
town forced themselves on our attention. They were all
trim, light, and soundly built, with gaily coloured balconies.

'German refugees,' said Mr. Balagiya regularly, over and
over again.

Then quite suddenly I noticed that we were driving down

[4] *Zellerbach Commission Report*, 1958, Section VI, p. 8.

the avenues of the spiritual wasteland that had been Camp
Valka. It was a nondescript sort of area now, mainly open
space, though there were a few familiar wooden huts among
the fir trees on the outskirts. 'German refugees,' said
Mr. Balagiya again, though with rather less feeling than
before.

Mrs. Berghaus, the counsellor, was sitting up in the back
of the car looking keenly through the windows.

'What a change,' she said. 'It is five years since I was
here. I wouldn't have recognized it. All over there—and
she pointed to a stretch of open space—'all over there were
wooden barracks. It was a foul place. It certainly looks nicer
now.'

Ahead of us appeared a line of barracks: long, low,
bungalow-type stone barracks with trim little gardens full
of beans and sunflowers and hollyhocks which gave the
impression of having grown there regularly for many years.
All seemed to be inhabited.

'What's this, then?' I asked Balagiya.

'What's left of Camp Valka.'

He parked the car and we got out. We walked down a
path between the barrack blocks and the sunflowers. Some
middle-aged women in cotton dresses were sitting in one
of the gardens. They took no notice of us. Balagiya stopped
about half-way down the stone block and knocked at an
open door. There was an invalid's wheel-chair parked outside
it.

It was a second or two before I realized that Balagiya
was talking to someone who was at the eye-level of a child,
but who was not a child. I had a glimpse for a moment of
the large, round head of a strong-looking man of about
thirty-eight, and then it disappeared again. By the time the
rest of us had reached the door Balagiya was alone there.
'He'll be out in a minute,' he said.

We were looking into a small, empty concrete hall with
two doors leading off it. Out of one of these doors towards
us now came the man whose head I had seen before. It was
still at the eye-level of a child. Where his legs should have
been were two thick leather pads, and he manœuvred himself

quickly on the pads towards us. One of his daughters, a child of about eleven, came to the doorway with him. She towered over him.

He had three children altogether. He was a Yugoslav taken prisoner during the war, in which he had lost a leg. After the war he had decided that Tito's Yugoslavia was not the one he had been fighting for so he had turned himself into a refugee. His name was Mehmed Karamovic. He had been here in Valka for eight years now, that is to say through all the years of its existence as an 'abomination'. One day he had been knocked down in a motor accident in the camp and had lost his other leg. Recently his wife had run away, leaving him with the three children.

He combed his hair so that we could photograph him, and afterwards showed us the two rooms. They were much like any refugee rooms. By now I was finding it difficult not to view such rooms as if they were some stage set. The potted plants seemed like standard props. I realized how difficult it must be, if you worked in this refugee world, not to accept these standard sets after a bit, so that the urgency wore off your awareness that something had to be done. This was where the danger lay. For in spite of all the theoretical talk I had heard about refugees wanting to stay in camps, the refugees themselves seemed to retain a magnificent urgency about their refusal to acquiesce.

Mr. Karamovic's rooms were better than many others I had seen in that at least they were soundly constructed of stone rather than of rotting wood. Here the roof was less likely to leak: here the sounds of everything that went on in the next room day and night were not, as in wooden barracks, part of one's own life. But here Mr. Karamovic was still a refugee in the place in which he had been a refugee for the past eight years. And as he looked up at Mr. Balagiya and asked if there were not some possibility of getting an apartment, the spirit of revolt in his face was very strong. Balagiya told me afterwards that Karamovic had said to him that he was at the end of his tether and was just beginning to drink.

'Note,' said Balagiya. 'Just beginning. After eight years of the worst refugee camp in Germany, just *beginning* to drink.'

Karamovic had admitted to him that during his momentary disappearance when we first arrived he had taken a nip to give himself the courage to face us.

I walked down the roadway counting the barracks on each side. Fifteen altogether seemed to be inhabited, not counting one with a police sign outside it. I walked into this hut and asked one of the policemen there how many refugees there were altogether in the barracks. He consulted a colleague.

'About 800 altogether I should think.'

'How many of them are foreigners?'

'Oh, most of them are foreigners. But if you want full details, why don't you ask the High Commissioner's representative here?'

'There's a High Commissioner's representative *here?*'

He told me how to get to his office.

'Thanks very much.'

'Representative of the United Nations High Commissioner for Refugees' was written on the door. Balagiya and I went in. A polite secretary said she would see if Mr. Terlin was free. Like all members of the High Commissioner's staff, Mr. Terlin, who was a very young Belgian, received us with a courtesy so immediate that it was as if it had arrived by sleight of hand. With these amiable people, it is not only as if nothing would be too much for them, but also as if their whole activity were dedicated to proving this.

'Good morning, sir,' he said. 'Now, what can I do for you?'

'Good morning,' I said. 'I wondered if you could tell me how many refugees you have here.'

'Altogether there are just over 300, but I could find out the exact number at once.'

He leant forward prepared to call for a secretary, treating even his desk with consideration.

'But the police here whom I've just spoken to say that there are more than 800.'

His expression was that of very clean plate glass.

'Here in Zirndorf there are just over 300 people.'

'Ah! No, I don't mean in Zirndorf. I mean here in Valka.'

'Valka is closed.'

Behind his back, framing his eager, polished face as he sat there, was a window. Through this window I could see a dismal stone barrack and Ukrainian and Polish women moving desultorily about their gardens.

'I beg your pardon?' I said.

'Valka is closed.'

'But I can see refugees walking about there just outside the window.'

'Valka is closed!' This time his voice rose to a slightly hysterical note.

'Well, who are those people, then?'

'The only refugee-reception centre is now at Zirndorf a few kilometres from here. There is no longer any Camp Valka.'

I tried to speak very calmly and slowly:

'Do you think you could please tell me how many people of the sort that I can see at this moment outside your window there are living in those stone buildings?'

'Ah, I see!' He made it sound as if I had been stupid and he was covering up for me. 'Of course.' And this time he rang for his secretary. She was back in a minute or two with the figures; and he read them out like winning numbers in a lottery.

'The total number of people in these stone settlements is 900. Of these 860 are foreign refugees. Of these 80 per cent., or about 730, are "homeless foreigners", or what used to be called "D.P.s."' There was a pause. 'Furthermore, I can tell you if you wish'—it was as if he were on to the consolation prizes now—'286 of these are children between the ages of six and fourteen. 150 are children between the ages of one and six.'

'But these people are not in Camp Valka?'

He looked puzzled, though still considerate.

'But I told you: Valka is . . .'

'Yes; I know. Thank you very much.'

It was impossible to get angry with such a polite man.

After this the rest of the day seemed rather an anti-climax, which proves how dangerous it can be to become familiar with the refugee scene.

At the side of a railway embankment on the outskirts of Erlangen we visited the 'home' of a so-called 'free-living' refugee, an Albanian who had somehow been deported to Germany for forced labour in 1941 and remained. We walked past some tipped rubbish and broken concrete blocks at the bottom of the embankment and in through a dark doorway. We stumbled up some even darker stairs. Half-way up there was an indescribably revolting smell, but it was impossible to see what caused it. The usual sort of situation awaited us at the top: two rooms with six beds for a mother and father and seven children. Only the mother was at home. She was expecting another child in a few months. There was no bed-linen. Filthy clothes lay piled on one of the five upright chairs. The man earned 80 marks (£6. 10s. 0d.) a week, a normal wage for an ordinary building labourer in Germany today. His children's allowances brought up his income for the family of nine to 520 marks a month (£43). The rent for this foul place was nearly £4 a month, and was about to be raised to £5. I stared dutifully round at the rotten, peeling walls and was glad to get out.

This time the light from the rooms revealed the cause of the smell on the staircase. I was glad to see that it was only a stinking overflowing pail of slops and garbage resting in the corner.

Outside Balagiya said that he had applied for a housing grant for this family under the special U.S.E.P. World Refugee Year scheme, but it would be a slow business. First you had to prove U.S.E.P. eligibility, which could take a long time. Then, if you got the grant, you had to find the apartment. Was it a better principle to look for individual apartments for such cases, rather than to build apartment blocks? Ideally, yes, everyone agreed, if you could find them, because in big apartment blocks, together with other refugees, the refugee identity tended to stick. I asked what sort of housing programme the High Commissioner's Office had for out-of-camp refugees.

'I don't think they know,' said Watson. 'I don't think they've got any plans yet. They're only just registering the out-of-camp people now.'

At lunch Balagiya said that the Deputy High Commissioner had written to him once to say that he had read in the Press a complaint of his (Balagiya's) to the effect that the High Commissioner was not doing enough for the Arab refugees in Tunisia and Morocco. Now the Deputy High Commissioner wrote to point out that in fact during the year $116,000 had been channelled through the High Commissioner's office for the benefit of these refugees. A lesser man than Balagiya might have been deterred by this. But he merely wrote back to point out that, as there were over 200,000 refugees in Tunisia and Morocco, this represented an average expenditure per head of just over 50 cents per refugee during the year. Watson laughed.

'Does that 50 cents take into account administrative costs, I wonder? If not, I shouldn't be surprised if each refugee actually gets a bill from the High Commissioner in the end.'

It was at lunch too that Watson quoted, with reference to the High Commissioner's office, somebody's remark: 'Well, I don't know a formula for success, but I do know one for failure, and that is to try to please everybody.'

After lunch, at Forcheim on the road to Bamberg we passed some two-storey apartment blocks which looked different from those being built everywhere else.

'Yes,' said Balagiya. 'They were built by the United States forces for refugees. And Mr. Watson's organization provided the furniture. I have a case I want to look into here. He is not in fact in these blocks any more but in a camp of "a-socials" a little further down the road.'

He explained the case: an elderly Yugoslav who'd been in a concentration camp under the Nazis; he and his wife had been given apartments in the new U.S. blocks but had fallen behind with the rent and had been thrown out. Now he was in this 'a-socials' camp and was going through a very bad time. 'They are nearly all German refugees there,' said Balagiya, 'and they beat him up. He's a sick man.'

'But why do they beat him up?'

Balagiya seemed to think my question a naïve one.

'He is not a German.'

The 'a-socials' camp by the dried-up bed of a canal didn't look any worse or better than any of the other camps I had seen. The only possibly identifiable 'a-social' element was by no means peculiar to a refugee camp: a girl in a white sweater and a blue skirt who stood about in a certain recognizable attitude in the doorway of a hut. There was a television aerial on the roof; also stones and old bicycle mudguards to keep the roof on in a high wind. A German refugee woman, seeing me with a notebook, came up and asked if something couldn't be done to get her out of there. She showed me round her filthy, peeling rooms stuffed with the beds and cots of her five children before I could begin to try and explain that I could do nothing.

Meanwhile, Balagiya had found that his 'case' had gone. The man had left the camp 'last Monday' for an apartment in the town. When he had first discovered the case, Balagiya had written to a charitable organization, the Christian Society for War Wounded, and now presumed that they had taken action.

'Case closed,' said Mrs. Berghaus, making a note in her files. 'But, of course, we'll continue to keep a watch on him.'

The incident suggested that a lot went on in the refugee world that never got near the High Commissioner's or anyone else's neatly roneoed and precisely worded files.

'Do you often find stray cases of that sort these days?' I asked.

Balagiya echoed the words Watson had used when I first questioned him about the High Commissioner's out-of-camp figures: 'Oh, yes. All the time.'

The particular Bamberg group of out-of-camp refugees who had been the first cause of our journey lived in a small stone building in a quiet quarter of the town. That is to say, the outside of the building was stone, but it seemed no more than the shell for a gloomy, rickety wooden and cardboard interior composed of staircases, partitions, and rotting floors at conflicting angles with each other, in the manner of some improvised contraption for the housing of rabbits or guinea-pigs. Families of former Soviet citizens from Azerbaijan and Turkistan lived here—100 of them

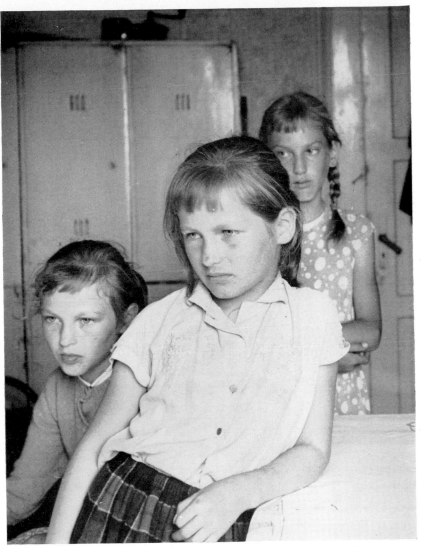

Yugoslav children in Camp Asten at the end of World Refugee Year (*see overleaf*)

The High Commissioner with a Yugoslav family (*see page 122*)

altogether. They crowded round us, showing us the usual rotting boards and the places where the rain came in. Unlike the German woman at Forcheim, they were un-impressed by my notebook. They had seen too many note-books brought out with the identical look of sincere concern on the writer's face.

'Ah, promises. Always promises!' said one of them bitterly.

A man called Mamedov, who had been living here for eight years, said he'd been to the Town Hall once or twice a month for years now, but he always got the same answer: 'We don't have enough room for our own people.'

'The Germans are against us,' he said with quiet fatalism.

A well-dressed Azerbaijani in a red shirt, check trousers, and sandals, who was visiting some friends in this building took us to see the single room which his wife and son occupied in a private house. It was dark and overcrowded with furniture, but seemed a privileged place after the sinister stone building where refugees scuttled and crept about the rotten interior. However, he had his own detail to add to the chaos of the refugee world. He had applied for a housing grant under the U.S.E.P. World Refugee Year scheme, but had been rejected for 'undivulged reasons'. He thought the undivulged reasons must have been something to do with his membership more than twenty years ago of the Communist Youth Organization, the Komsomol. Mrs. Berghaus confirmed that such membership quite often disqualified refugees for assistance. That this should be so was made ridiculous enough by the fact that most of these former Soviet citizens from Azerbaijan and Turkistan had joined the Wehrmacht to fight Communism during the war. But what made it particularly ridiculous in this present case was that the man in the red shirt had now been working for some time on a United States Army base. He had had to obtain U.S. security clearance, for this job of course, but the United States Escapee Programme had had to conduct their own security clearance, and on this they had failed him. So this refugee was in the peculiar situation of being simultaneously both accepted and rejected by a United States security clearance scheme. It was unfortunate

G

for him that he happened to have been accepted for the work, but rejected for the assistance. A further complication of course was the obscurity as to whether it was his Communist or his Fascist affiliations that he was rejected for.

U.S.E.P., in the opinion of both Watson and Balagiya, had done admirable work for refugees, but was also just as riddled with bureaucratic red tape as the rest of the refugee world. Balagiya quoted the instance of a Bosnian who wanted to practise as a doctor in Germany, and, having passed his first medical exams, had applied for a U.S.E.P. grant to subsidize further studies. A student committee had testified that he was an exceptionally good student and that it was highly desirable that he should be able to complete his studies. The grant had, however, been refused by U.S.E.P. for the reason that the man was technically eligible for emigration and therefore could not receive help under a non-emigration World Refugee Year scheme. The fact that he had no wish to emigrate was considered irrelevant.

Of course, hide-bound rules of one sort or another are necessary in the administration of any ordered scheme. The rules for the working of U.S.E.P. are laid down in America by the State Department in a world very remote from that of the refugee.

'But how awful,' I said to Watson, 'sometimes to have to apply such rigid rules here on the spot in the refugee world itself.'

Watson stared non-committally into the middle distance.

'Yes,' he said, with the complete lack of emotion which made his comments telling. 'Although, from what I've seen of most of the U.S.E.P. people, they're well—pretty U.S.E.P.-minded.'

The rest of my impressions of that day consist almost entirely of fragments of Watson's conversation as we drove back to Munich.

'. . . I'm very much opposed to specifically political or denominational help to refugees really, and nearly all the voluntary agencies are, of course, of one denomination or another. The Churches have certainly done the most wonderful work among refugees, and I was drawn to this sort of

work from the religious point of view myself, but if only
they would provide the money without strings attached. . . .
You know, there's actually been a case of a Catholic getting
up at a conference and saying he couldn't recommend help
for unmarried refugees living together. . . .

'. . . I've seen U.N. counsellors who are just thick from
the neck up. I don't know how to describe them. They're
just clots. . . .

'. . . Of course, a lot of people compare the refugee
situation with that in other parts of the world. Hong Kong,
for example. They say this is really nothing here because
the numbers are so much smaller. But I don't agree with
that. The point is that the suffering here is really far more.
For the refugees in Hong Kong, though their conditions
are far, far worse than here, there's hardly any difference
for them from their normal surroundings. The same is
true of the refugees in Pakistan. But it's when you take
people out of their environment that you have the true
refugee problem. Hong Kong and Pakistan are really often
problems to which a refugee label can only be technically
attached. . . .'

And as all the way home we flashed past block after block
of new apartment houses which, in spite of all the multiple
refugee machinery, were not being put up for those few
thousand refugees who had been 'out of their environment'
now for fifteen years, it seemed to me more than ever that
this unambitious, unemotional, ordinary English voice was
one of the few voices of sanity in an otherwise chaotic and
heartbreaking situation.

IX

All the different nationalities among the refugees in Germany have their own national committees. During a morning
spent in Munich before moving on to Vienna, I went to
visit Mr. Michael Rudko, head of the United Ukrainian

Relief Committee. He was a youngish, middle-aged man, balding a little, with a gentle face and a soft voice. As soon as he knew that I was British, he said:

'First, I must tell you how really very grateful we are to the British people who have given us so much help through the British Adoption Committee. This is real, concrete help. In fact, I would say that as far as we Ukrainians are concerned the effectiveness of the help given by the Adoption Committee in this way has been greater than that of any organization.'

'Including the High Commissioner's Office?'

He spoke very calmly:

'Including the High Commissioner's Office.'

I said:

'I do rather get the impression that the effective work on behalf of refugees is not proportionate to the size of the terrifically complicated machinery working for them, or to the vast amount of money that is put into it one way or another.'

Again Mr. Rudko spoke very calmly:

'That is my opinion too.'

Altogether, he said, there were about 14,000 Ukrainian refugees in Germany, of whom 6,000 were in need: 1,000 of these were in camps. About 5,000 Ukrainians in need were living out of camps, although this was only an approximate figure as he hadn't finished registering them all yet. I asked why more of those in camps, like Alexander Terlecki and his family, hadn't been able to take advantage of the recent British mission.

'In my opinion,' he said, 'that British mission was here much too short a time. It did not have time to visit camps and find people. And we had not had time to prepare people for it. In fact, we put forward four families, but two of these were rejected. I don't know why, though it was probably what are called political reasons. I don't know what we can do about this. I don't know whether we can appeal against this decision or not. We are very much in the dark. One thing I cannot understand: the parents of the wife in one of the rejected families—the Zaleski family—

are already in England, living at Ashton-under-Lyme!
Why cannot the daughter and son-in-law go too? Mr.
Zaleski is a healthy man of thirty-five, working as a driver.
His wife has had T.B. but is cured now. And there is no
background of crime. . . .'

He talked about some of his out-of-camp refugees:

'Many of these people are living in an awfully bad situation, working for German farmers for 60 marks [£5] a
month with full board. They are split up in ones and twos
all over Germany and it is often very difficult to reach them.
For some of them their situation is not so different since
they were first brought here. I will tell you about one old
woman. She is sixty-three now. She was brought here with
her two sons in 1942, but she long ago lost track of them,
and has no idea where they are. In summer she works for
a farmer from four-thirty in the morning until ten o'clock
at night. He uses her practically as a slave. And yet what can
you do for her? You can't send her to an old people's home.
She would hate that. As long as people can work and want
to work, you can't do that. She said to me herself: "You
know, I've been working here for so long; I can't change
now. I know the farmer here is a very bad man. But here
I have my cows. And even if I have no work to do I go to
these cows, because no one understands me any more
among these people, but these cows do. . . ." '

Here Rudko stopped for a moment. 'She speaks very little
German, you see. I thought at first when she said this:
she is not normal. But it was not true. When she started
to talk at greater length and told me her whole life-story,
I saw that she was perfectly normal. She went on to say:
"You see, I don't know what kind of people these are here.
That is why I want to stay with my cows; I do know them.
I think I will stay here as long as I can, and probably I will
die here, and that will be the solution for me." '

For the out-of-camp refugee in cities, he said, it was
important to remember that the problem was not just to
find them decent housing, but also how to help them pay
the rent. He knew of many cases of families who had been
helped with money from U.S.E.P. to get a house, but had

received nothing to pay the rent with, and such people were often in difficulties. He had, he said, a case at the moment of a family in trouble because they couldn't pay the rent. They were due to be evicted in a day or two and had nowhere to go. Would I like to see them?

He sent for one of his full-time counsellors who knew the details of the case. We set off together to visit the Pancio family in the outskirts of Munich.

The building in which the Pancios lived was a decent-looking one. The counsellor told me that they had one room there in the five-room apartment of a German landlady.

We went into the building and up a clean stone staircase to the first floor where we rang a bell. We might have been going to visit a modest but comfortable member of the European middle classes in any city in western Europe.

A neatly dressed youngish woman with an intelligent face opened the door. I automatically assumed that it was the German landlady.

The counsellor introduced her as Mrs. Pancio.

She led us along the corridor to a light, smallish room overfilled with beds and cupboards, and with slops and rubbish piled in a corner by the stove just as in a refugee room in a camp, except that the solidity of the walls, the absence of damp, and above all the knowledge that the room was not in a camp made it seem infinitely more cheerful.

Mr. Pancio had taken the two-year-old child out for a walk and Mrs. Pancio was busy with the lunch while the baby slept. But she showed no sign of resentment at our intrusion, and in fact seemed grateful to have someone to talk to in the family's terrible predicament. She took a saucepan off the stove and turned out the gas.

Mr. Pancio was forty-eight. He was born in the Polish-administered Ukraine, and had been taken to Germany as a slave labourer in May 1940. At the end of the war he had become a refugee, and had worked first as driver with the Bayerische Motorenwerke for four years. Then he had a bad stomach illness, and this put him out of work for two years. It also made it impossible for him to emigrate, which he would have liked to do. Towards the end of this period, in 1952, he had met his wife, and they had lived together in their present room with their growing family for eight years. He had been able to take up work again, and had been a taxi-driver in Munich until February 1959, when he had again fallen ill. He still couldn't work. The family of four had been living on social welfare of 267 marks [£22] a month ever since. They had to pay 25 marks rent for their room, but had never once failed to pay it. The German landlady wanted her room back for herself (she had four rooms for four people at the moment), and had taken the Pancios to court seven times in four years in an attempt to get them out. Each time the court had decided in favour of the landlady, but at the same time had issued a stay of execution, in view of the fact that the family were refugees and unable to find other accommodation. Now, however, the humane resources of society were exhausted. Mrs. Pancio put the latest document in the case on the table in front of us.

It was signed 'Dr. Murenwald, *Amtsgerichtsrat*,' and dated Munich, 19 July 1960. It outlined the main details of the case, stressing the fact that a stay of execution had now been granted seven times, and concluded:

'However true it may be that the defendants are now— as they contend—in a state of economic need and in no position to obtain for themselves alternative accommodation, there cannot, in spite of the plea for a further stay of execution, be any question of postponing the eviction any longer.'

The eviction would take place in two days' time.

'Where will you go?' I asked Mrs. Pancio.

'We have nowhere. Into the street.'

In spite of the tone of Dr. Murenwald's letter, I couldn't believe that in this Germany of the 'Economic Miracle' a mother and father and two young children could simply have to live in the streets.

'Oh, no,' said the counsellor. 'Of course, they could go to institutions for the destitute. But the family would be separated there. The mother from the father and the children from the parents.'

The tears which suddenly came into Mrs. Pancio's eyes

were particularly disturbing because up till now she had been completely composed.

'No,' she said desperately. 'I cannot be separated from my children. They can't take my babies from me.'

'What can you do?' I asked the counsellor.

'We will ask Mr. Watson for 3,000 marks with which to buy the lease of an apartment. That way, by putting the money down, you can get a cheap rent, perhaps 90–100 marks a month, although actually the rent is not so important here, as I think we will be able to get the German welfare to pay it. But in the meantime . . .'

I turned to Mrs. Pancio.

'Haven't you got any German friends you could go and lodge with while he tries to get you an apartment?'

She looked at me in astonishment.

'No,' she said, as if stating a most obvious fact. 'We have no German friends. Our only friends are other Ukrainian refugees.'

'But surely . . . After all, you've been in Germany twenty years now. . . .'

'Nevertheless, we're still strangers. We're last class citizens here.'

If a dominating or hysterical woman had made this comment, one might have been inclined to dismiss it as emotional bitterness. But from this quiet, modest balanced woman it carried a terrifying conviction.

'Would you still like to emigrate, then?' I asked.

'Of course,'

'Would you go to England if you could?'

'Of course we would.'

'They're such *decent* people . . .' said the counsellor as we went down the stairs. Even his case-hardened mind seemed to have found something particularly distressing here.

Of all the refugees I visited in Germany, none made me more ashamed of my inability to do anything but ask questions than Mrs. Pancio. This did not seem the moment to ask the counsellor why something hadn't been done to find the family alternative accommodation on one of the other occasions when the case had come up in court and a stay of execution had been granted. One could only be grateful that something could probably be done so desperately late as this.

In the refugee world Munich has something of the atmosphere of a seaport. It is a headquarters for many national and other voluntary organizations, and every sort of individual refugee story can be found there. Here more than anywhere else you feel that you are not looking at a refugee problem so much as a whole refugee way of life. In Munich it is a matter of course to run across in one day two cases so utterly different as those of Dr. Kotsovsky and Eugene Danchenko.

Dr. Kotsovsky is a Rumanian Professor of sixty-four who had been a prisoner of the Russians in World War I. In a Russian prison camp he had received a head injury which was later operated on. It left him with a severed facial nerve and badly distorted features. In spite of this handicap, he rose to be head of the Institute of Gerontology in Rumania between the wars and the owner of a private clinic. During World War II he was sent by the Germans to be Director of Health in Odessa. He fled before the advancing Russian armies, first to Vienna and then to Germany. After the end of the war, he worked in American and American-run hospitals in Germany and later in U.N.R.R.A. and I.R.O camps. He was then at the height of his powers, but he was also a 'handicapped' refugee, and that meant that for him life must now begin to run down. When I.R.O. came to an end, he found a room in the camp in Moosacherstrasse, Munich, the camp in which the Polenskas and the Pumyczs lived and which the High Commissioner had said was not a camp at all.

Professor Dr. Kotsovsky was luckier than the Polenskas or the Pumyczs. In 1956 he and his wife found a room in a council house at No. 8/iii, Pragerstrasse, Munich. There he has lived ever since. There a year ago his wife died.

Now, despite his circumstances, Dr. Kotsovsky had never lost his passionate interest in his own particular branch of medical science. He had written two books on more general subjects, *Dostoievsky, Tolstoy and Bolshevism* and *Tragedy of the Genius* (the latter was published in Munich in 1959), but most of his writing continued to be on gerontology and in his lifetime he has published more than 250 articles on the subject in medical journals all over the world. For all this he needs books. Though he now lives only on his German social welfare allowance of 120 marks [or £10] a month, his only complaint is that this does not allow him to buy books, though some periodicals and current medical journals do reach him through friends.

But all he really cares about is reading and so, since the death of his wife, a new problem has developed. For Dr. Kotsovsky lives very much like the traditional absent-minded professor. He hardly needs any furniture. He has sold most of what he and his wife had, to buy books. And as a result, his room has become hopelessly untidy, and he has been threatened with eviction because of the state in which he keeps it.

Fortunately, the High Commissioner's representative has here been able to exercise his watchdog function with effect. Dr. Kotsovsky has been bought furniture, which he still doesn't really need, and he will be protected from eviction.

Eugene Danchenko is a Russian of twenty-two. Until 18 October 1959 he had been a Soviet border guard, stationed near Berlin. On that date he crossed over to the freedom of the West. When I saw him, he was living on a special temporary settlement of the Tolstoy Foundation just outside Munich. An official of the Tolstoy Foundation drove me out to see him.

On the way this official and I talked of the usual refugee problems, particularly housing. A little way out of Munich we passed a large complex of many-storeyed apartment blocks.

'See those?' my companion said laconically. He was an American of Russian extraction. 'Ludwigsburg, this place is called. All those blocks were built with Marshall Aid and I.R.O. funds given to the German Government to help

house foreign refugees. But at least half the people living in
them are now Germans.'

I asked if we could make a detour. We swung half a mile
or so off the road. Inside the spaciously laid-out, tree-lined
avenues we stopped. Some obviously un-German-looking
faces were staring out of a window.

'They look as if they come from one of the Chinese
republics of the Soviet Union,' he said, like any specialist
identifying an unusual specimen.

I asked him to ask them if there were many Germans
living in these apartment blocks. A resigned, cynical expression seemed to come into their faces as they answered.

'They say that at least two-thirds of the people living
in these blocks are Germans,' he said.

We drove on to see Eugene Danchenko. He surely could
hardly have had time to develop a cynical view of the
freedoms of the West.

But although Danchenko was happy and comfortable
enough in the excellent Tolstoy Foundation settlement in
which he was now installed, he had already been through his
period of disillusion. He was a solid, chunky young man with
an intelligent, extrovert face. He would have made a good
Rugby football forward or, later in life perhaps, an effective
American politician.

Immediately after crossing the border, he had been taken
to Düsseldorf, where he was screened by the British military
authorities for two months. He had no complaints about
that. He saw that it was a necessary measure, and he had
been well treated by the British. But after that he had been
taken to Camp Valka.

Valka was then not even closed in the High Commissioner's eyes, but was functioning as an official reception
camp for incoming refugees. This was in December 1959
and Danchenko had stayed there until February 1960, two
years after the Zellerbach Commission had described the
camp as an 'abomination' and had recommended that
in the interests of the West it should be closed as soon as
possible.

'It was a terrible place to arrive at,' he said. 'I tell you I said to myself: "What have you done, you fool?" I bitterly regretted ever having become a refugee. For in the Soviet Union the conditions at the worst'—and he repeated—'at the *worst*, were better than at Valka . . .'

One day he had been beaten up by the police there. It was a typical incident in the camp's regular pattern of disorder and gangsterism and squalor. '. . . I was walking home one night back from Nuremberg to the camp, when I was stopped by some police in a car on the road just near the camp. They asked me for my papers, and when I produced them and they saw I was a Russian, they just beat me. It was typical of the everyday atmosphere of the place. . . .'

The Tolstoy Foundation had rescued him and brought him to Munich, where he now had a job with the Munich radio earning 410 marks [£35] a month. He paid 135 marks [£11] a month for his board and lodging.

'Now that I've been here six months, I'm quite impressed by the West. And, of course, I am very glad now I came. But, apart from what happened to me at the beginning, it is very terrible being kept waiting around so long, as I am now. Oh, I know I have a good job and this place here is very nice, but I want to get on with my life. Why must the emigration be so slow? I tell you, for people who have torn up all their roots this uncertainty is very terrible. Because for you it may just be slowness, but for us it is uncertainty all the time. . .'

He wanted to go to America, and he probably would be accepted in the end, but as the U.S. law stood at present it looked as if he would have to wait a year and a half. In the meantime he was writing his life-story and he had met a Czech girl refugee he wanted to marry. All in all, he was probably quite happy. And yet there was a restless look about him, a flicker of anxiety about the eyes which didn't fit at all with the sturdy frame of the Rugby football forward— a progressively undermining sympton of the 'uncertainty' of which he had spoken. As we left him, I couldn't help feeling that it was the West and not himself that really had cause to be made anxious by his experience. Just before I went I repeated:

'And you're quite sure that, except for this waiting, you're now certain you made the right decision?'

'Oh, yes,' he said with something like solemnity.

It was reassuring.

My last call that day was on a large, ample-hearted, charming, middle-aged Swedish lady who spoke English so well and so sensibly that it came naturally to mind to say that she had her head well-screwed on. She was Ella Larsen of the International Rescue Committee, Chairman of the Council of Voluntary Agencies.

I asked her about the apartment blocks at Ludwigsburg. She confirmed that they had been put up for homeless foreigner refugees and that they were now largely inhabited by Germans.

'But why can't the High Commissioner take this up with the German authorities?' I asked.

She shrugged her shoulders. *92090*

'I have taken it up myself with the German authorities more than once. But all they have said is that there are no "homeless foreigners" needing housing!'

She wanted to make clear that bureaucratic delay was not confined to the High Commissioner's Office.

'Now take U.S.E.P.,' she said. 'As you may know, they have a special World Refugee Year project for all refugees—that's to say, which is not confined to those normally within the U.S.E.P. criteria. . . . Well, I submitted my first cases for this project as long ago as last February, and now, five months later, I still haven't had a single answer!'

But the High Commissioner's office did not escape the weight of her quiet, yet powerful rebuke.

'Yes; they are late in coming round to the problem of the out-of-camp refugee. And then, again, I wonder why is it that they are only concerning themselves with those in Baden-Württemberg and Bavaria. Why are they not for the moment doing those in North Germany at all? . . . Ah, Valka. Yes; I know. You see, the High Commissioner regards those people in the stone barracks there as integrated within the German economy—it's not even an unofficial camp. I have frequently put it to the High Commissioner that for the people who have been in those barracks for eight years when Valka was so bad, it is still psychologically bad, but . . .'

She had a story of the days when Valka was in all senses bad. A Czech border guard—a Czech equivalent of Danchenko—on patrol one day had shot a refugee who was trying to escape from Czechoslovakia into Germany. When the guard had come up to the body of the man and had seen him lying at his feet, he had been suddenly overcome with traumatic horror at what he had done. He had immediately thrown away his rifle and come across the border himself. He had been put in Camp Valka.

But the traumatic shock had endured. The man became temporarily deranged. Though derangement resulting from sudden mental shock can be relatively easily dealt with by immediate psychiatric treatment, the man had been allowed to wander around Camp Valka for three years without any medical treatment at all. At the end of that time his condition had deteriorated to such an extent that he was probably incurable.

There must, I reflected, be many people now integrated within the German economy at Valka who remembered him drifting past the sunflowers in their gardens.

It seemed to me time to go and see if they managed these things better in Austria.

AUSTRIA

X

The office of the High Commissioner for Refugees in Vienna opens off a long, hygienic, L-shaped corridor in the same expensive, lift-filleted building that houses offices of the German and Indian embassies. To obtain admittance to the corridor you must ring a bell, and a man comes and politely asks your business, as in Belgrave Square. In the room occupied by the High Commissioner's representative, a photograph of the High Commissioner himself hangs on the wall, just as if he were in fact a head of state.

All this, you may feel, augurs well for the position of the refugee in Austria, since he is obviously represented at diplomatic level on an imposing scale. On the other hand, you may also contrast the impressive, aseptic surroundings with the foul barracks in which refugees live, and you may feel that there is something obscurely wrong. These may be emotional irrelevant thoughts, and certainly any member of the High Commissioner's staff will be quick to tell you that they are, with the peculiarly clean brand of sweet reasonableness of which they are masters.

Apart from impeccable politeness, it is this exceptional cleanness of body and mind that distinguishes any member of the High Commissioner's staff. Physically, they might have been spun from the purest nylon and often it is as if their minds contained some fine, deodorizing spray which magically dissolves the smells and other realities of refugee work into what they otherwise recognize to be a matter of the greatest urgency and importance.

I was therefore interested to hear that my guide through the refugee world of Austria was to be an Australian member of the High Commissioner's staff. It did not seem possible that there could be such a thing as a nylon Australian.

I was to be proved right. But Bill McCoy seemed to begin

badly. He arrived with devastatingly polite punctuality at my hotel to say that he was afraid he himself wouldn't be able to accompany me to the Yugoslav transit camp at Trais-kirchen after all. Of course, he had arranged for someone else to go with me instead, and we would call in at the office for briefing on the way. I asked him if camp-clearance in Austria really had any hopes of being completed by the end of 1960.

'Plans for camp-clearance', he said, 'will have been com-pletely drawn up by the end of this year; and many of them will be in process of implementation. There will, of course, be certain residual groups in the camps after that time.'[1]

Somehow this sort of thing sounded worse than usual in a barely perceptible Australian accent. A few minutes later the substitute arrived—a Mr. Jackson from the Legal Department—and I postponed my judgement on whether or not there could be such a thing as a nylon Australian.

We drove to the High Commissioner's office. On the way Mr. Jackson, a tall, young, bespectacled Englishman with a slight foreign accent, outlined some of the aspects of the present Yugoslav problem. The causes of this inflow of some 400 young Yugoslavs a month had been explained to me in Salzburg by Arthur Foster. The great practical problem, as far as Jackson was concerned, was to decide: (1) whether these were genuine political refugees and therefore within the High Commissioner's mandate, (2) whether they were simply economic refugees and therefore not within the mandate, and (3)—if (2)—what was to happen to them? ('For the High Commissioner says: "Though not concerned, in accordance with my mandate, with people who are not refugees, I have a humanitarian interest in them."') Looking rather fixedly far ahead through the windscreen as if he were just about to bite his lip Jackson admitted that up to November 1959 over 50 per cent. of all new incoming Yugoslav refugees had been sent back to Yugoslavia. The figure was now about 10 per cent.

[1] Cf. Mr. Felix Schuyder, new High Commissioner for refugees, on February 1, 1961: 'It was hoped to complete camp clearance in Austria during 1961 and that all remaining camps in Europe would be cleared in 1962, although a few very difficult cases might still be left pending conclusion of their solutions.'

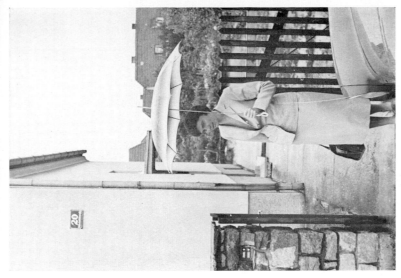

Miss Freko

'. . . we have a lovely home, but no house
to put it in.'

Hong Kong refugees

Traiskirchen was the camp where all incoming Yugoslav refugees were at present held by the Austrian Government—whether accepted as political refugees or not. 'Nowadays, *any* refugee—whether political or economic—can be sure that, *once he gets to Traiskirchen*, he will not be sent back.'

'But I thought you said if they were economic refugees they couldn't be accepted.'

'The legal position is at the moment a little tricky.'

It seemed that a certain amount of humanity was now agreeably confused with the legality. The position was roughly as follows:

If a Yugoslav came over the border and reported to the police there were three possibilities. Either he was recognized as a political refugee. Or he was immediately expelled. Or he was permitted to stay pending emigration. The form this permission took was a formal expulsion order, coupled with a stay of execution (*Vollstreckungsabschiebung*), and most of the Yugoslav refugees in fact enjoyed this precarious status.

'During this time the economic refugee is technically in *Schubhaft*. . . . *Schubhaft*, you see,' he said, with a nice feeling for the language, 'is the *Haft* you're in pending the *Schiebung*.'

I nodded.

'Now the man who comes in illegally is *prima facie* liable to expulsion. The crossing of the border illegally is, of course, an offence.'

'Of course.'

'What I mean is that for the pure political refugee it is *not* an illegal offence, because Article 31 of the Geneva Convention says that no person coming from the country of persecution shall be punished for any illegal border crossing. But for the economic refugee the illegal offence is illegal. Which is why he gets Haft and not Asyl.'

I was beginning to enjoy this refugee dialectic almost as much as Jackson.

'But now what about the people who are expelled immediately after crossing the border?'

'Well, where the refugees are plainly criminal elements, the screening and expulsion takes place locally.'

H

'But who is to say that they are criminal elements?'

'Well, we have our own man covering Klagenfurt and Graz, and if he doesn't agree with the police decision then the case *must* be referred to the Ministry of the Interior. Apart from which, *all* rejected cases have to be referred to the Ministry of the Interior anyhow.'

'Of course, local police forces sometimes have a way of acting on their own initiative.'

The thought seemed unthinkable to Jackson's legal mind.

'But the Decree of 29 March 1959 says that everyone *must* be put through the eligibility procedure.'

With talk of writs of *mandamus* and *ultra vires* we proceeded along the early morning streets of Vienna to the ambassadorial offices of the United Nations High Commissioner.

There, a quietly electric man in a blue suit named Ken Elliott filled in some of the rest of the Austrian refugee situation.

Figures were available with their usual rather implausible precision. There were 51,065 refugees within the mandate in Austria; 5,500 of these were in camps, 1,200 of them Yugoslavs; 575 were in institutions; 990 were in unofficial camps, and about 45,000 were living out of camp. They were at present making a proper registration of the out-of-camp refugees.

I remembered Foster's complaints. No only about the Yugoslav economic refugees, but also about foreign-speaking refugees who had been given Austrian nationality by naturalization and were thus automatically omitted from those figures.

'Ah, one minute, please,' said Ken Elliott. 'It is quite true that many mandate refugees did receive Austrian citizenship and are therefore not within the mandate any longer. Altogether 300,000 were naturalized. But you must remember that here in Austria *Volksdeutsche* (ethnic Germans from Eastern Europe and Yugoslavia) came within the High Commissioner's mandate, and most of these 300,000 were *Volksdeutsche*. They are in the main not at all badly off. They know the language. They are by nature more industrious than many of the foreign-speaking refugees. They are, after all, pioneer settlers by tradition. For instance, many *Volksdeutsche* have formed themselves into communities and built their own houses without any help from anyone. Whereas, on the other hand, the foreign refugee has perhaps come to expect help.'

'How many of these 300,000 were *not Volksdeutsche* then —were in fact foreign speaking refugees or old D.P.s?'

'The figure of 300,000 former mandate refugees now naturalized includes 30,000–50,000 foreign-speaking refugees. But don't think these have been left entirely without help. Some of them did get help in spite of their naturalization, because the help had been approved before the Austrian citizenship actually came through. Then as to those still in camps there is an Austrian Government camp-clearance programme parallel to our own, so they will not be forgotten.'

I told Ken Elliott that I had seen Arthur Foster.

'Oh, Arthur is a good man, a humanist,' he said sincerely. 'But the people he should get at are the Executive Committee—not us!'

I remembered what Arthur Foster had said about the delegates to the Executive Committee. ('They don't know a bee from a bull's foot'.)

'What's Camp Asten like?' I said, remembering Foster's description of it as 'a hell-hole'.

'Material conditions are quite good there,' said Ken Elliott in a nice, balanced way. 'It's the psychological aspect that's not so good. . . . Now, Parsch in Salzburg, that does give you the creeps.'

'I wonder if I could see them both?'

'Of course. You can see absolutely anything you like.'

Jackson and I lunched together in the village of Traiskirchen before going into the camp. He took the same precise care over the ordering of his lunch as he did over explaining the legal status of Yugoslav refugees.

He told me that the same sort of circumstances which had caused the present residual European problem to persist after most of the old D.P.s had been resettled was repeating itself all over again with this new influx of Yugoslavs. He cited the case of a Yugoslav who had escaped and succeeded in getting to Canada. He had arranged with his wife that once he had successfully emigrated and found himself a job he should send her word, and she should try and escape too with their child. He sent word, and she escaped successfully. But when she arrived in Austria it was found that she had T.B., and she was not allowed to join her husband. Already perhaps, a new 'hard core' nucleus was being assembled in this way.

Jackson also told me a less usual case history. A refugee who was a homosexual had emigrated to the Dominican Republic, but had been expelled for his activities. Austria, as the country of first asylum, was bound to take him back. In Austria he had been several times convicted of 'unnatural offences', and the Austrian Government, losing patience, decided to send the man back to his Iron Curtain country of origin. They were entitled to do this under the article of the Geneva Convention relating to refugees which permits forced repatriation for 'particularly serious crimes' rendering a man 'a permanent danger to the community'. Jackson, as representative of the High Commissioner, saw the man in prison and got him to agree to see a psychiatrist. The psychiatrist, after examination, said that, under treatment, the man would eventually prove curable. Whereupon Jackson pointed out to the Austrian authorities that though the phrase of Article 33 referring to serious crimes might appear applicable, they could not invoke it to justify his expulsion, since, if he were curable, he would not eventually be a permanent danger to the community. Jackson's legalistic dedication secured the refugee not only a reprieve, but free medical treatment as well.

It was perhaps too easy to forget that this sort of mind was as valuable to the refugee world as Arthur Foster's.

Traiskirchen Camp had been a military academy in the days of Hitler, and after the war a barracks for Russian occupation troops. Basically, therefore, it was a solid, roomy,

and Spartanly healthy sort of establishment, and it had
been thoroughly cleaned and redecorated after the Russians
had left. From the outside, with its parade ground and
flagpole and properly laid-out three-storey buildings, it
looked a reasonable enough place to be a reception camp for
refugees.

A man met us at the gate. He looked a little like a Feldwebel
in the Luftwaffe I had known. He said:

'*Ich bin der* Camp Leader *von dem* Free Camp.'

Was there then a camp here that was not free?

He gave me the sort of look I might have expected from
a Feldwebel. Of course not. Everyone was free here.

What then, I asked, had he meant by 'the free camp'?
It seemed to presuppose another camp that was not free.

After a brief inner struggle, he seemed to remember that
he was not a Feldwebel.

Look, he said. What he had meant was this: He was the
camp leader of the first two floors of these buildings. Up on
the third floor was the processing or screening stage, through
which all new refugees must pass on arrival. That was
nothing to do with him at all. That was under the control
of the police. There were 156 people up there at the moment.
Yes; they were locked in. They stayed there perhaps a
week on the average or perhaps a little longer. There were
about 1,000 people in the camp altogether. Now was I
satisfied?

We walked into a large hall, where behind a sort of pen,
like a sheep-dip, were about thirty men, women, and
children. All had about them the quite different hard, brown
look of people who have recently spent a lot of time in the
open air. Some of the women had handkerchiefs tied round
their heads; one wore a long green skirt and gold earrings.
She had two little boys with her, about eleven years old.
Most of the men were in their very early twenties and wore
suits with open-necked shirts. All had come across the border
from Yugoslavia within the last day or so. They looked
grateful to be allowed just to sit there while clerks took
particulars and issued them with knife, fork, spoon, bowl,
and blanket.

'They will be quite glad of the rest up on the third floor', said the camp leader with paternal sincerity.

We moved up to the first floor to see how those who had had their rest were getting on. Many of them seemed still to be resting in the big rooms divided by cardboard partitions that rose no more than about half the height of the ceiling. In one of these, three boys, all wearing suits that were now rather crumpled, rose politely from their beds. They were all nineteen years old. They seemed quite pleased to answer questions. It was like being an officer going around barracks and asking if there were any complaints.

'Oh, no; it is much better here than in Yugoslavia. . . .'

'Except that it is rather dirty here. . . .'

'And we would very much like to work. . . .'

'We have nothing to do but hang about all day. . . .'

'Though here, of course, there is much more chance of getting work than in Yugoslavia. . . .'

I asked a fair-haired boy why he had come.

'Economic refugee,' he answered, pat, with a certain serious pride, like a schoolboy who is learning a new subject. 'I was working in a quarry, but there was so little money. . . .'

Another, with a round, brown face and dark hair said even more proudly:

'Political refugee. I had to join the Communist Youth.'

'But why didn't the other one have to?' I said, nodding towards the fair boy.

'He probably would have had to some time or other.'

In another room, smaller but unpartitioned and thus complete in itself, I found a mother with three small children. Yes, she said, it was all right here, but why did they have to wait so long? They wanted to emigrate to Australia. Her husband had been here nine months already. Yes; she had left Yugoslavia later. (Here another woman, who was with her, put in: 'She carried her children over the frontier.' The mother smiled modestly.)

I asked what they had done about trying to get to Australia. She said they had announced their wish to go. They were told that their wish would be put before the Australian

Commission and they just had to wait. They were waiting. But, of course, waiting here was better than Yugoslavia.

The 'camp leader' had been carefully unobtrusive throughout these interviews, as if our skirmish over the definition of freedom at Traiskirchen had made him decide to play his hand differently. Most probably he didn't think of himself as having a hand to play at all. Anyway, he now seemed to judge the moment ripe for a word on behalf of the authorities.

I mustn't think, he said, that everyone had to wait here a very long time. Only in exceptional cases did people have to stay here as long as six months. Between one and four months was the average. Perhaps I would like to see the Austrian who was in charge of the documentation here? He would be able to give me an exact picture of the emigration situation.

The man in charge of documentation was a tired, sincere man, unusual in his profession inasmuch as he was obviously more interested in human beings than in paper. 'Yes,' he said; 'it was all terribly slow. It was a pity that World Refugee Year was now coming to an end and everything was still moving so slowly. Now take these Yugoslavs—it was only Canada and Australia that seemed interested, and even so, things were moving much more slowly than they need. It would help, of course, if the migration commissions could come here directly and work on the spot. At the moment the refugee had to go to the Commissions and, of course, that meant that if he were at work he would lose his pay. This was the sort of thing that slowed things up.'

I asked if the voluntary agencies who were the refugees' link with the migration machinery had offices here.

'No; but each voluntary agency usually visits Traiskirchen once a week. They come on different days.'

'Wouldn't things move faster if the voluntary agencies had permanent offices here?'

'Oh, undoubtedly. At present, of course, there are two permanent representatives of the United Nations High Commissioner here every day, but they are not directly concerned with the migration machinery. They are establishing whether or not the refugees are political or economic refugees and generally safeguarding their status.'

'You said that only Australia and Canada were interested in taking Yugoslavs. Do you think if England were prepared to take them, any would want to go?'

'Unfortunately the English have no programme for these people. Most of the refugees want to go to Australia or Canada, but certainly some would want to go to England if they could—say as many as 10 per cent. After all, the most important thing for refugees is to begin their new life as soon as possible. It is the gap in between the two lives that is the painful experience.'

Compared with the old refugees, for whom the gap had lasted sometimes fifteen years, I realized that these new-style refugees at Traiskirchen were receiving princely treatment. And yet, with the memory of that fifteen-year fiasco in mind, it seemed a terrible thing that, if the delay were in fact avoidable, these young people should continue as 'refugees', in the painful sense of that word, even a day longer than necessary. Four months could seem a very long period of uncertainty to a boy of nineteen who had no family to communicate with, and who was deprived of all the moral support of the surroundings in which he had learnt to live. Of course, it was quite possible that there was difficulty in securing immediate transport facilities through I.C.E.M., and that this was the real cause of the delay. I decided to suspend judgement until I had interviewed the I.C.E.M. authorities in Salzburg, an appointment which, I had been told, would be made for me by Bill McCoy.

Meanwhile, we strolled about the tall, bare corridors and staircases of this former military palace of the Third Reich, confirming that its present incongruous inhabitants were, in their fashion, glad to be there.

'Of course', said a small man in an open-necked white shirt, whom I stopped at random, 'some of the rooms are very overcrowded, but otherwise there's nothing really to complain of.'

We went into one of the large 'family rooms', divided up into cubicles by flimsy partitions reaching about half-way

up to the ceiling. Here there was even less privacy than
existed in the old barrack-type refugee camps, where at
least families had whole walls to themselves, however thin.
This laterally bisected warren must have been a strange
place for young people to sleep in at nights.

But the chief complaint of the mother of four children
whom I found there making clothes on a sewing-machine
was the delay itself rather than the conditions in which it
was experienced.

'I have a brother in Canada, but it doesn't seem to help.
Three months ago I gave in our names to go to Canada,
but we have heard nothing. Yes; here we have enough to
eat. But we do not have enough clothes. I make what I can
for the children, but it is hard. No; we are given no clothes
here, and small children need clothes.'

She bent over the sewing-machine again industriously
but with a certain gaiety. Talking to these Yugoslavs was a
quite different experience from talking to the old refugees in
the camps. With the people who had been in camps for fifteen years or so, one was awkwardly aware that they were
in some way 'different'. One felt cramped, in spite of a
determination not to be, by the feeling that they deserved
special consideration. Here no such frightening, invisible
barrier had yet had time to erect itself. These refugees of
a few months were still just part of a non-refugee world.
For them the label 'refugee' had not yet acquired the
sinister ring of the leper's bell.

And yet there *was* something special about the last two
new refugees whom I saw in Traiskirchen, even though
they had been there for a much shorter time than most of
the others.

True to character, the Camp Leader had shown us round
every bright, scrubbed pot and pan in the immaculate
kitchen, had let us glimpse an anonymous soup simmering
in its giant cauldrons, had ostentatiously questioned a member of the kitchen staff about the number of grams in the
meat ration. As he lead us amiably but firmly towards the
hospital, my heart sank. The hospital, he said, was particularly well equipped, and he would like us to assure ourselves

of the excellence of the installations. Had he been a different
kind of man, I would have suspected him of trying to get
his own back for the fuss I had made at the beginning. We
shook hands with doctors and heads of departments, asking
all the questions about their activities which it would have
been impolite not to ask. The door was opened on a dentist
busy with a refugee patient, and we seized the excuse to
withdraw without further inquiry; but the dentist followed
us out, leaving his patient open-mouthed in the chair. We
visited a number of rooms in which uncompromisingly
efficient sterilizing apparatus was in use; Jackson took
advantage of the fact to have a boil on his arm cleaned up.
Finally, the camp leader said:

'There are two old people I want you to see upstairs.'

We went upstairs and walked through an empty ward
which for some reason struck me as sad and sinister, as if
the blankets and pillows were heaped up on all the beds
because the last of their occupants had died. At the far end
a small room led off from the main ward. On a bed there
an old man in a waistcoat and trousers, with no collar, and
an old woman, knitting, sat close together side by side.
Both had bare feet.

The old woman's legs were crossed, and one foot, swollen
and clean and pink, waved very slightly backwards and
forwards as she knitted. When she saw us she smiled through
eyes that seemed swollen in the same sort of way as her
feet. She only stopped knitting for a moment to nudge
her husband, who was sitting bolt upright in a gentle
doze.

They were Czechs, or, rather, Czech *Volksdeutsche*. He
was eighty. She was seventy-eight. Ten days ago they had
been living as they had lived for the past twelve years under
Communist rule in Czechoslovakia. Out of the blue the
authorities had come to the old man and told him that he
must work on the harvest. If he didn't, his pension would be
stopped. The old couple had nothing but their pension to
live on. The enormity of the idea of compelling an old man
of eighty to work suddenly seemed to both of them the last
straw. So they decided to get out at last, and made their

way on foot for two days and nights across the mined and
heavily patrolled frontier.

The work on the harvest itself would have been child's
play for the old man compared with the demands of the
escape itself. But that had not been the point. It had simply
seemed to them intolerable to threaten a man of eighty with
starvation if he didn't work. So they had got up and walked
out, treating the society which could treat them like that
with contempt.

The old man had been a groom in the days of the Austro-
Hungarian Empire and had worked in Vienna for a time.
Later, he had been a postman. Suddenly, he was struggling
to stand upright off the bed. He couldn't quite manage it.
'*Hoch Österreich!* (Up Austria!)', he cried. It was as if
the forces that prevented him from rising were somehow
the same as those he was so defiantly challenging. His wife
took a hand from her knitting and put it affectionately on
his knee. '*Hoch Österreich!*' he repeated as we said goodbye,
but this time he didn't try to rise. He just sat there con-
serving his strength for the life ahead. His wife smiled and
went on with her knitting, which was of far more interest
to her than any casual visitors.

XI

The largest group of refugee camps in Austria lies around
Linz. The majority of these camps are not 'official' camps,
but the hypocritical distinction between official and unofficial camps is less important here than in Germany. In
Austria the unofficial camps are included in the High
Commissioner's 'camp-clearance scheme'. In Austria the
deceptive use of terminology applies to people rather than
places. For although the innumerable little groups of rotting
barracks to be seen at almost every turn on a journey round
the outskirts of Linz, are all at least officially camps, the
families in them as often as not will be 'naturalized Austrian'

refugees and thus, from the High Commissioner's point of view not officially refugees. Though these families will be eligible for the Austrian Government's own camp-clearance scheme—which only began in 1959—the fact remains that any picture presented by the High Commissioner's office of the 'progress' in this area underestimates the real suffering among refugees.

'You've no idea,' said a High Commissioner's official to me in the Linz office, 'how many people come to this office and say, "we hear you're distributing apartments. Can we get on the list?" We ask them: "Are you refugees" They say: "Yes; of course we're refugees." Then we say: "Have you Austrian nationality?" And they say: "Yes." And then, of course, they begin to realize what a big mistake they made in applying for Austrian nationality some years ago, because we can do nothing for them.'

Half an hour later, as we drove out to Camp Asten, we passed Camp Ebelsburg on our left, inhabited mainly by former D.P. refugees who had taken Austrian nationality. Ebelsburg had been built by Hitler twenty years before. It wasn't necessary to visit it to know what conditions there would be like.

Camp Asten itself still preserved something of the macabre grandeur of the Third Reich. An arched and turreted gateway built by the Nazis in 1939 still stood at the entrance. Beyond it stretched the main camp street, with dingy improvisations masquerading as shops (*Frisur, Kantine,*) and dismal acres of damp wooden barracks on either side. Borders of empty bomb-cases had been erected at intervals to give to patches of waste land a grotesque, municipal dignity.

This visit to Asten was to be different from my visits to other refugee camps, for I was not outwardly an official visitor. Fräulein Barbara Freko was a good-looking, placid twenty-nine-year-old girl who worked as a Camp Counsellor for the German Catholic voluntary agency, *Caritas,* and she agreed to take me with her on what was to all intents and purposes one of her ordinary routine rounds of the camp. She was someone whom the refugees took for granted in

their everyday lives, someone to whom they came with
their troubles, their good news and their bitterness, whom
they trusted because she knew their world from the inside
and not through a wall of invisible but tangible glass.

We had hardly entered the main street of the camp when
a very angry-looking, middle-aged man put his head up
from behind a hedge and stared at us. Then he turned
abruptly away. It was difficult to tell whether his air of
general hostility had been directed specifically against us
or had just happened to sweep over the hedge in the moment
in which we passed. But this very doubt conveyed to me
something of the atmosphere in which a counsellor had to
work in such a place. I looked across at Miss Freko as she
walked along the road beside me. She was looking calmly
down at the road, though I knew that she had seen the
man. I wanted to ask her why that man had looked angry,
but it would have been like interrupting some highly skilled
technician in his handling of a delicate machine. Instead I
simply said: 'I suppose you know most of the people here
by sight?'

She nodded. Then after a pause she said:

'You know, in some ways it is not the people in the camps
who are worst off. It is the old people living out of camps
who are really in a bad way. I don't know whether you
know, but the Austrian welfare rate for two people is
520 schillings (£7. 5s. 0d.) a month. That is below the
level of subsistence. I simply don't know *how* such people
live.'

We passed a hut in front of which two little Jewish boys
in caps with long, straggling hair were playing.

'There are about sixty Jewish families in Asten,' said
Miss Freko. 'These very religious Jews won't go to Israel,
of course; they disapprove of Zionism. The American
Jewish voluntary agencies look after them here and keep them
supplied.'

'But why don't they fix them up with housing?'

She shrugged her shoulders. For her the sight of Jewish
people still in 1960 living in camps built by Hitler had no
special significance. It was simply one more part of the

accepted day-to-day situation with which it was her job to deal.

A small, dark man was coming down the road towards us. Miss Freko stopped him. His apartment was all fixed up, she told him; he could move in two weeks' time. Though he had been living in camps ever since 1945 and had a wife and children, he seemed to take the news as if it were just a routine piece of information.

'Oh, he knew he was getting an apartment quite soon,' said Miss Freko as we moved on. 'He just didn't know exactly when.'

'Even so I would have expected him to be a bit more excited.'

She shrugged her shoulders again.

The mixed smell of cooking and latrines which I remembered from the camps in Germany came across the road towards us. The dilapidated wooden barracks here, stained with time, seemed as bad as any I had seen.

'Oh, they are good compared with some,' said Miss Freko. 'You see, the roofs on that block are quite sound.'

A sudden gust of wind blew across the empty space in front of us, entangling strips of paper in the stalks of the long weed that grew there. We walked across to a group of three young women who stood in the doorway of a hut surveying the scene as women in a densely built area of a town will survey a street. They were all Yugoslavs, like most of the population of Asten. None of these three had been here long by European refugee standards. And thinking this, I realized how dangerous it was that one should be able to think that two years or one year in such a place was 'not long' to be a refugee. These were the new refugees, last year's or the year before's counterparts of the people I had been seeing in Traiskirchen. Could it be that the whole sickening, complacent business of the last fifteen years was beginning all over again?

'This is a horrible place,' said one of the women. But she spoke with the relative cheerfulness of someone who could still think of her surroundings as temporary. 'There is nothing good here. And nothing to do but wait to go.'

Meanwhile, her little girl was going to Switzerland for a holiday on Monday, which was something. Miss Freko said she would be helping to escort the party.

But for one of the other women things were not so easy. She and her husband hadn't yet applied to emigrate, because their two small children were still in Yugoslavia. 'As long as they aren't here we'll stay, but the moment they come we'll go. She is right: there is nothing good here.'

I asked Miss Freko what could be done about trying to get the two children out of Yugoslavia.

'Well, we are trying,' she said in the same calm way as she had accepted the angry look from the man behind the hedge.

'Now,' she said as we moved on, 'I will show you someone for whom I can do nothing.'

The old lady was a *Volksdeutsche* from Rumania who had come to Austria in 1940. She was seventy-two and had been living in camps for twenty years, nine of which had been spent in Asten. Miss Freko could do nothing for her, because she had taken German nationality. Relatively speaking, she was not badly off, since her husband had been a Government official and she got a widow's pension from Germany which was higher than any Austrian pension would have been. She even received us in a certain *bourgeois* style and offered us tea. She had two rooms, she explained, going into details of her accommodation with a certain pride, as is the habit of old ladies. This was the room she used in summer because it was on the corner of the barrack block and was cooler. But in winter she moved up to her other room in the centre of the block, where she lost less heat. Oh, yes, she had to pay for both—60 schillings (about 18s.) a month they cost her—but it was worth it and, of course, now there were more rooms available in the block.

'Of course, you know,' she said, 'what is really so bad is that one can hear every word that is said through the walls. And there is so much drunkenness and swearing. . . .'

Coming from someone who was so much better situated than all the other people I had heard voice this complaint,

it irritated me. I looked across impatiently at Miss Freko
to suggest that it was time we moved on.

It was then that a curious sound revealed that though the
old lady was still trying to talk, something had gone wrong.
One moment she had been sitting there, demure, even a
little priggish, discussing the uncouth behaviour of the
neighbours she had to put up with, and the next her whole
fragile frame was shaking with sobs. The deep furrows on
her face ran with tears. The words were all out of control.
It was as if a small child were crying: 'Oh, if only I could
have a small apartment . . . just a small apartment . . . it
has been so terrible here all these years. . . .'

She cheered up a little when we let her show us her
other room. It was very stuffy and still in there, like in a
front parlour that is seldom used. The same quiet, solitary
potted plants stood in corners and religious pictures hung
on the walls. The elaborately embroidered coverlet on the
bed looked as if it were spread there for some special guest.
But, of course, the guest would be herself.

Moving away down the corridor through the rank, damp
smells and past the peeling walls, there seemed something
almost miraculous about the happy faces of the children
who came running and skipping down it towards us. Several
of them attached themselves to Miss Freko and came out into
the sunlight with us. Two other small boys saw Miss Freko
from across the open space and hurried towards her.

'Please, Mummy says: "What are we to take with us on
Monday?" '

'Just some washing things and a change of shirt and some
socks and handkerchiefs. Not more than you can carry.'

They too were going on the holiday party to Switzerland.

'Please, who's going with us?'

'I'll be going with you.'

Only one child of our Pied Piper procession was still
with us as we approached the next hut—a very small boy of
three or four who twined himself round Miss Freko's leg
when we stopped. Gently she unwrapped him and sent him
back to play with the others. We went into the hut.

'I have got a Croat family in here who will be going off

to Canada tomorrow. They didn't know they were going
till yesterday.'

Everyone in the room seemed to be moving diagonally
across it from one half-filled suitcase to the other at the
same time. A month-old baby in yellow blankets lay on a
bed beside bundles of clothes and linen. A small boy,
in a check shirt, sat on the end of it. His mother said
apologetically that he wasn't feeling too well because
of his vaccination. She stopped her business-like dashes
across the room to fetch a bottle of some syrupy dark
wine, like cough mixture, which her husband poured out
with hospitable ceremony. He alone seemed completely
calm.

Oh yes, he said, he was pleased to be going, but he was
a little anxious. He had been here so long now—fifteen
years. His wife was very pleased, though, because of the
children—there were five of them altogether. It would be
good for them in Canada. Years ago he had had T.B., but
it had long been inactive. He was going under a special
Canadian scheme for the sick. 'What's good about this
scheme,' he said, 'is that you don't have to pay anything.
You see, under the old emigration schemes, where the fare
was paid by the voluntary agency, you had to pay it back
gradually once you got there. But you can't tell how difficult
life is going to be when you get there, can you?'

He would be taken to hospital as soon as he arrived in
Canada to make sure that his T.B. was properly cured, and
his wife and children would be provided for until he was
able to look after them himself again. He was a skilled
shoemaker. He pulled out a reference from his employer
which said that Josef Subić had been an excellent worker
and could be trusted with any sort of work.

I asked him if he had tried to emigrate before.

'In the old I.R.O. days it was hopeless,' he said. 'No one
who had had T.B. had a chance. There was no sense in
trying. In 1956 I tried to get to America, but they discovered
my T.B. history, and I was rejected. Then later the same
year I tried to go to Sweden, but Sweden said I wasn't ill
enough. . . .'

I

We sipped some more of the cough-mixture wine. A friend from next door came in to share in the excitement. He seemed slightly drunk already.

'Yes,' said Mr. Subić, 'I won't say that I am not anxious. How do I know I shall be able to earn my living in Canada? Everyone says it will be easy, but I don't know that. I do know that I can earn it here. Still'—he looked across at his wife busily piling up her pillow-cases—'she will be glad. And I expect I will too. The important thing is freedom. Freedom to say what I like and to work where I like. That's all that life is really.'

As Miss Freko and I got up to go the slightly drunk man stood up too, suddenly belligerent.

'And what about me, eh?' He came very close, with a slightly cork-screw action. 'You are English?'

'Yes.'

'On 9 May 1960 I was up before the English Commission in Camp Wegscheid. But they wouldn't have me.'

I could think of nothing to say. Then I remembered the new Swedish Commission that was said to be around somewhere in Austria.

'But I don't want to go to Sweden. I won't go to Sweden.' Equally suddenly he dropped his belligerence. 'I don't know where I'm going,' he said desperately. 'I don't know whether I'm going forwards or backwards, left or right. . . .' He was like a character in a Chekhov play. The Subićs smiled indulgently as he retreated towards the bottle, and we were able to leave with the comfortable illusion that everyone was happy.

Outside a wind had got up. Curtains billowed out of open windows like washing hanging on a line.

'I want to show you a family I'm very fond of,' said Miss Freko.

But on our way to their hut we were stopped by a tall, handsome, blonde woman holding a little boy by one hand and a yellow ball in the other. She had a sophisticated, city face. Her husband was a book-keeper from Ljubljana. Had Miss Freko had any news yet of their fate with the New Zealand Commission?

Miss Freko had heard nothing. I asked when they had been up before it.

'A month ago.'

'Oh, well,' I said, looking at Miss Freko, 'I expect that's quite a reasonable time to wait, isn't it?'

Miss Freko didn't answer, but asked if she'd been up before any other commissions before. She said that Canada, Australia, the United Kingdom, and Sweden had rejected them since they first came to Austria as refugees in 1957, but they had rejected them without giving any reason. Each time the commission had written simply saying that they were rejected. She said goodbye to us politely, as if we had simply been unable to tell her the way somewhere, and walked off a strangely elegant figure with her little son, more suited to a fashionable beach or a shopping street than this mouldering waste land, and yet, with true dignity, somehow not ill at ease here either.

I asked Miss Freko why the migration commissions couldn't give the reasons for rejection to the refugees.

'They just never do,' she said calmly.

The Arnautovic family had been in Austria since 1945, and had lived in the same room at Camp Asten since 1947. There were eight of them altogether now: mother, father, five girls, and a boy. The father was an unskilled labourer, and was still out at work when we called. But the mother, and the children who had known no other home than this overcrowded room, were a fine example of the principle that, if a family is in itself a happy one, cramped conditions do not necessarily have a harmful effect. Which is not to say that such conditions are not extremely unpleasant and that people living in them don't long to escape from them.

Two of the Arnautovic girls were going on the excursion to Switzerland with Miss Freko. They discussed the problems of luggage together. It was difficult not to sit there bemused by the natural dignity and resilience that had made these little girls so bright and intelligent and polite. It was not as if, like the Polish family I had met in Germany at the official camp of Neckargartach, they had the advantage of an upper-middle class, 'face-preserving' tradition to support them. This was a simple peasant family, and though their tradition had no in-built provision for the unnatural strains of slum life, it had survived with equal nobility.

Wanting to pay some tribute to the quality in this family which they themselves took completely for granted, I made a stupid mistake. I complimented Mrs. Arnautovic on the tidiness of the room and the prettiness of the children's clothes.

She delivered the rebuke humbly enough:

'Just because you're poor, you don't have to be dirty.'

I asked if I could photograph them, and they agreed.

'Please just carry on talking quite naturally,' I said as I brought my camera up to my eye.

Mrs. Arnautovic smiled—for the first time, I thought, a little wearily.

'Oh, yes,' she said; 'all the photographers say that.'

Some weeks later in Geneva I was shown a happy picture of the High Commissioner for Refugees sitting jovially in a group with a 'typical' refugee family. It was the Arnautovic family. Only it must have been taken well over a year before, because the youngest member of the family then was now the youngest but one. The Arnautovics had, of course, been rejected for migration by various countries, including Australia, the United States, and the United Kingdom, long long ago. Would there, I wondered, ever be a point at which the patience of such a family would break?

It was now late in the afternoon, and Miss Freko looked at her watch as we strolled slowly back up the main street of the camp towards the turreted gateway. A car from the High Commissioner's office in Linz was coming to pick us up in about half an hour.

'You see that man over there,' she said suddenly, 'that man sitting on that bench?' I saw him. 'Well, he's one of the worst cases we have here.'

A youngish, languid-looking man with a sallow face and long rather elegant black hair, and wearing a brown suit and dark glasses, was sitting on the bench by the side of the road. He was savouring the evening air and the sight of the strolling passers-by just as if he were sitting lazily at some café table on a pavement. But there was also about him something which I recognized from my days in a wartime prison camp: an air of consciously prolonging ease and time to a point where few others could follow. The expression on such people's faces conveyed that they were assuming their idle enjoyment of the passing hours as a right, as part of the natural dignity of man.

'He's a Rumanian Jew. About thirty-five, I think. He's been here since 1947, and he simply won't do any work. He once took a job for a short time, but he dropped it when he realized that he wouldn't get his unemployment benefit any more. He just lives on that now and on some help he gets from time to time from the American Jewish agency.'

He welcomed us with an infinitely lazy, old-world Jewish charm which was just recognizable as politeness. Slowly he smiled and shifted along the bench. Miss Freko sat down beside him. He smiled at her under his dark glasses, turning his face round in what for him must have involved a major effort. He had one elbow thrown loosely over the back of the bench, so that his hand dangled idly in front of it at a point very close to the upper part of Miss Freko's bare arm. Slowly his long fingers began to caress her flesh. Equally slowly, while still talking to him, Miss Freko lifted his hand away. He went on smiling beneath his dark glasses.

At fifteen he had been put into a Nazi concentration camp, and had spent four years there. He had been liberated by the Russians in 1944. Perhaps it was his escape from extermination that he had been savouring ever since.

Miss Freko was asking him why he didn't get a job again. 'There's time,' he said. 'Plenty of time. *Ich hab' immer Zeit.*' He managed to say this in a way which gave the phrase considerable distinction.

Slowly his long fingers began to caress her arm again. Again she dealt with him admirably, removing his hand in such a way that, although she removed it firmly, the gesture was almost flattering to him. To me she muttered in English: 'I wish I'd sat down on the other side of you.'

I asked him if he had ever thought of going to Israel. 'No,' he said. 'It's too hot there.'

But did he really want to stay here for the rest of his life?
'Plenty of time,' he said. 'I would like to go to Africa one
day.'
'But Africa's even hotter than Israel!'
He shrugged his shoulders.
'*Immer Zeit.*'
He was more interested in Miss Freko. Again I saw her
gently shift his hand. He smiled at her.
'You are a beautiful woman,' he said. 'The most beautiful
one here.'
She repeated that it was time he got a job.
How the transition took place I am not quite sure, but a
moment later as he turned to her there was a quite different,
agitated expression on his face.
'Tell me, then, why do they persecute me when I work?
I work and they take my money away from me, so, of course,
I don't work.'
Miss Freko explained the absurdity of expecting unem-
ployment money when working.
For the first time his whole body displayed a surprising
energy:
'They passed a special law to take my money from me.
Just against me. Tell me why do they pass this law against
me. It is unjust. A special law, a *Sondergesetz.* . . .'
From this more serious assault Miss Freko disentangled
herself seriously, pointing out the unreasonableness of his
demand as if it were simply unreasonable and not absurd.
Soon the anguish of persecution had left his face and he was
pressing the complaint only as a matter of form. He smiled.
Miss Freko stood up before he could stroke her arm again.
'I think you ought to go to Israel,' I said. 'It's a wonderful
place. I think you would like it there.'
He treated this statement with the contempt it deserved.
Clearly he would have hated the ostensible extrovert bustle
of modern Israel.
'*Immer Zeit,*' he replied.
He waved us goodbye without getting up, and when I
looked back at the bench half a minute later he had for-
gotten all about us. He had lit a cigarette and was watching

the smoke drifting slowly along the street in the still evening
air.

Miss Freko was already talking to a young middle-aged
woman who was coming down the main street from the
gateway with a man of about her own age on her arm. The
man was holding a basket with a bottle in it. They both
looked exhausted.

'How is everything?' asked Miss Freko.

'*Schlecht.* Bad,' said the woman.

The man began to talk in a desperate, emasculated whisper
so that I couldn't understand what he said at all. He held his
head at an awkward angle all the time, as if trying to avoid
something.

The woman asked when they would be able to get an
apartment.

Miss Freko said she didn't think it would be long now.
She talked to the woman for a time, while the man stood
there with his head hanging lopsided, like the bottle in the
basket. Then the man and woman walked away. There was
a desperate attempt at cheerfulness on their faces.

Miss Freko hoped to get a small, semi-detached house
for them soon. Their case was so wretched that it would
have been unwise to put them into an apartment block with
the other refugees. They were Hungarians who had been
living in Yugoslavia, and they had been refugees twice in
the last six years, having escaped first to Hungary from
Yugoslavia and then from Hungary to Austria. In Yugoslavia the man had been imprisoned for political reasons
and had been tortured by being hanged until he was almost
dead. His vocal chords and his hearing had been destroyed.
He could get no work. They had two children, one of whom
had been born in Camp Asten.

As we walked out through the gateway, refugees were
streaming past us into the camp. Buses were stopping on the
main road outside the camp, dropping refugees who had
been working in Linz or had gone there for an afternoon's
shopping. Several trudged along towards the gateway with
satchels and brief-cases. Many waved to Miss Freko as they
passed us. She pointed out an elderly lady with grey hair

which seemed tied up in curlers and whose feet were obviously causing her pain as she walked. She seemed unable to control the angle to her line of direction at which she put them down.

"She must have been into Linz to do some shopping. That's why she's so tired. But I won't talk to her, if you don't mind, because she always gets so upset. She's Russian and used to be an opera-singer in Moscow. She was deported for forced labour during the war. Her husband was Jewish and was killed in a concentration camp, so she gets compensation from the German Government and isn't too badly off. She'll be getting an apartment in a few weeks' time. . . . But she still does get so upset.'

The car was late, and it was only while we sat on the grass bank by the side of the road waiting for it that I discovered that Miss Freko was a refugee herself.

She and her mother and father were Germans from Yugoslavia who had come to Austria at the end of the war. For years they had lived in an unofficial camp in Linz. Her father had worked as a carpenter, and her mother had worked on the roads, while she herself had got a job as a nurse in an American Army hospital.

'We were lucky, of course. I mean, I was lucky to get that job, because I had no training, and in it I was able to learn English, which has helped me a lot. And then my father was lucky that he was a professional carpenter and used to that sort of work. My uncle, for instance, who was a refugee with us, was a doctor, and manual work was too much for him. He died after a few years.'

'How did you get out of the camp?'

'We were determined to get out of it. We worked and worked, all three of us and saved money as hard as we could all the time and eventually were able to build our own house.'

'But surely you needed to save an awful lot of money for that.'

'Oh, we didn't do it all at once. In fact, it took us ten years altogether. It's really only just finished now. We bought the ground one year—that was in 1950. Then we started working on it—at week-ends. We could only work on it at week-ends, because we were all busy earning money during the week. We built the foundations the next year, the outside walls the next, and so on. We moved in in 1953—long before it was finished. Half the rooms weren't properly built, we had almost no furniture, and, of course, nothing was painted. But we had the roof on and we moved in. We had blankets instead of doors for quite a time. . . .'

At last I understood the almost unfeeling calm with which she was able to face much of her work among the refugees at Camp Asten. It wasn't only that she herself knew the life so well that she could take it for granted. But she wouldn't have been human if, in the circumstances, she hadn't also felt, somewhere, the very faintest contempt for those who had not managed to get themselves out of such a place.

There was nothing arrogant about her, though.

'. . . When I started counselling, I sometimes used to get so depressed by the cases that I thought I couldn't stand it any more. But I wouldn't do any other job, though it's not well paid. I love it. . . .'

She sat on the grass, watching the straggling home-comers trudging past her.

'Of course, still, sometimes, I have to get up and leave the room when things are too bad. . . .'

A motor-bicycle roared past us towards the Nazi gate-way, drowning her words. Its refugee owner crouched lovingly over the handle-bars as if he had been longing for nothing else all day but this return to the squalid barrack at the end of it.

'. . . You know, I can still remember how horrible it was in the camp when I had been on night duty in the American hospital. I had to try and sleep during the day, but I never could, because there was so much noise all the time. And then if I shut the window to try and keep the noise out, it would get so hot and foul in the room. And, anyway, the noise came through the walls.'

Our car drew up and we climbed in gratefully. It might have been carrying us back to another world. But it was impossible to forget the one we were leaving, even if we had wanted to. Dotted about on the skyline or set back from the roads as we passed, or lurking on waste ground in the suburbs of Linz itself were the disguised dark brown clusters of wooden huts to which thousands of other refugees, all of whom counted themselves lucky, were also going home.

XII

There are moments in life when the need to protest takes priority over reason. Very often the protest can later be harmonized with reason and made doubly valuable. Even if this doesn't happen, the protest may at least set other, more reasonable people thinking afresh. But in the moment in which the need to protest is first felt it is overwhelming.

It was Bill McCoy's bad luck that I had reached this stage by the time he came to Linz to take me through Upper Austria to Salzburg. I was by now disgusted with the fact that the progress of the refugee situation in Europe was, after so many years and after so much apparent attention, still so painfully slow in terms of human experience. The situation as I had found it at the end of World Refugee Year simply did not seem good enough. And in a fairly amiable, rationalized but emotional way I let him know this. He had heard it all before. He proved himself no nylon Australian.

A dark, medium-sized man in early middle age with a gift for Service-type slang made more effective by his native accent, he was as unlike a member of the High Commissioner's staff as one could expect a member of the High Commissioner's staff to be.

He came on the lunchtime train from Vienna. I had spent most of the morning seeing the more successful side of the refugee picture in the vast new townscape that was growing visibly out of the once notorious 6,000-strong refugee camp at Haid. I had seen a fine new school, rows of small houses, decent three-storeyed apartment blocks with yellow, pink, and blue balconies—all making the site look as if the odd groups of mouldering wooden barracks which were occasionally dotted about it were really things of the past. I had talked to an old man and woman in one of the apartments whose eyes had glistened with tears of joy as they told me how different their present life was from the old one here (once when they had lived sometimes as many as twenty-two people to a barrack room and five people to two beds). And yet the effect had been to make me think not so much of this progress since 1951, but of the numbers of refugees I had seen with my own eyes still living in conditions almost as bad in the second half of 1960. Later, in the morning, in another camp, I had found a tough little nut of an Englishman in a green windcheater who had been in charge of a group of English students helping to build and repair houses for refugees.

'There are infinite possibilities here for building houses for refugees in this way,' he had said. 'If only more voluntary labour could be organized. . . .'[1]

And when I had asked him why the local Council, to whom the refugees paid rent for their barrack rooms, didn't do the repairing, he had replied:

'There are a lot of people round here who might be doing a lot of things, but it's no good telling an old lady whose roof is leaking that the Council ought to have mended it.'

'Oh, I know,' said Bill McCoy over lunch. 'Sometimes it all simply drives you up the wall. You want to smash right through it. Don't think I don't feel like that too. It's clear to poor, blind Freddy that some of the ways you have to set about things are ridiculous, but in the long run it's *Monsieur le délégué de sowieso* you're up against. . . .'

'I beg your pardon?'

'*Monsieur le délégué* for some little place who gets up in Parliament and wants to show that he's keeping an eye on the way his constituents' money is being spent. After all, we can't do anything without the money that's voted through

---

[1] His own enterprise was part of a United Nations Association scheme. He was working with technical students from Southampton University who had contributed half of their own fares and keep.

people like him, and, of course, he wants everything to be properly hedged round with qualifications and conditions, etcetera, to prevent waste and too much expense generally. It's the attitude of mind you get with responsibility for money, and the betting is *Monsieur le délégué* probably is not, incidentally, the most clued-up person you could find on the refugee situation. So that when you're told that Country X will be taking so many bow-legged beekeepers from Bulgaria or Country Y so many blue-eyed Latvians you have to get on with it, though you may have hundreds of other refugees you'd like to resettle first and the only bow-legged Bulgarian beekeeper you've ever heard of happens not to speak a bloody word of Country X's language. . . . Then, again, people criticize *us* because we ourselves lay down restrictions and qualifications, but if you don't get enough money then you must have restrictions about the way in which you spend the money you do have.'

'What do you think of the criticisms that the High Commissioner's offices are overstaffed—your one at Vienna, for instance?'

'Sheer bullshit, frankly. I'm really sick and tired of having to answer gratuitous bloody criticisms like that all the time, that are directed against us rather than the situation. As I say, people go on as if we were satisfied with the refugee situation as it is. Of course, we're not satisfied, but this is the way things are. This is the way it has to work. The answer I can never get out of chaps like you who criticize us all the time is: "What would you do?" '

'Well, if this is how things are, then it's up to the High Commissioner to change things.'

'But *how*?'

'Well, he should resign if countries don't alter their immigration criteria or don't give him more money. Or he should get tougher generally.'

'He is tough. And what's the use of resigning, for God's sake? Somebody's got to do the job.'

We were to run down a number of cul-de-sacs of this sort in the course of the next few days. I could understand his point of view. Whether you liked it or not, this was the system, and all you could do was to work it as effectively as possible. To have a lot of emotional outsiders sniping at you all the time when in fact you worked yourself very hard indeed was almost intolerable. Bill McCoy's especial quality was that he didn't sanctify the system and try and pretend that its deficiencies didn't exist. He spent his time trying to get round them. And yet perhaps there may have been moments when even he was subconsciously glad that there were deficiencies to get round.

'It all requires a bit of fenangling, you know,' he went on cheerfully. 'You have to see if you can't get a few things by under the wire. . . . And, of course, at times it's not at all easy to know what *is* the best thing to do. I mean, for instance, what *do* you do with some old codger—say, a Russian Colonel of the 44th Siberian Hussars or whatever, who's been a refugee since 1920 and whose one pleasure in life is getting plastered? Do you go through all the rigmarole of trying to get him into an old people's home and all the rest of it? Well, I don't know but my solution would simply be to leave him where he is and present him with a couple of bottles of vodka once a week. . . . Then, again, outsiders with the best will in the world, who try to help, often get you into the hell of a situation just because they *don't* know how it all works. For instance, I don't know whether you remember in Ronald Searle's book that drawing of an old Hungarian refugee called Paul Weisshaupt?'

The name brought the picture to mind immediately. It had taken up a whole page of Ronald Searle and Kaye Webb's Penguin pamphlet, *Refugees 1960*—a squat, determined, isolated figure in a crumpled, out-of-date uniform, wearing a tall black fur hat, his pudgy fingers planted philosophically on the knees of his old breeches. A former officer of the old Hungarian Army, he lived in a tiny, dark room in the camp where he had been since 1945, suffering great pain from an unhealed wound which he had received in a motor accident in 1956. 'Sometimes,' he said to the authors, 'I wish God would take me. . . . When I get as hungry as a wolf I make some soup.'

'Well, an American woman who saw the picture reproduced

in *Life* magazine got in touch with me and said she would like to provide him with a small amount of money for the rest of his life. Fine. But in the meantime he'd been moved from the camp to an old people's home, where, because everything was paid for, the miserable pension he'd been living on was enough to give him a tiny luxury or two. But, of course, understandably, if he's in receipt of a private income, then he ceases to be eligible for his pension. So there's your problem. Here's this American woman whose conscience makes her *really* want to do something for refugees, and yet unless you're careful it'll end up with her simply paying a small regular subsidy to the Austrian Ministry of the Interior. . . .'

Late that afternoon we drove into the calm, unostentatious country precincts of the show-piece refugee sanatorium at Thalham, half-way between Linz and Salzburg. A short, middle-aged German doctor in a spotless white overall, with little round spectacles and the tubes of his stethoscope looping from his pocket, welcomed us with a clinical courtesy that was almost hypnotic. He took us into his surgery and began to talk at once in an unhurried, even tone about the establishment and its patients. There had been a sanatorium at Thalham for refugees since just after the war, and he had himself worked in it almost from the start—of course, the present place, with all its clean, light buildings and up-to-date equipment was hardly recognizable as the place it was then. There were 106 patients there, special chronic or bad tubercular cases, all refugees from 'almost everywhere you could think of between here and Vladivostok.' The sanatorium was under the administration of the Austrian Ministry of the Interior, and had been partly equipped with High Commissioner's funds. Ten of the patients were cases of severe mental disturbance. Something about the way in which the doctor gave me this last piece of information suggested that these were cases in which he had a special interest.

'By chronic cases I mean, of course, incurable. Some of the mental cases may prove curable.'

'What can you really do for a chronic case?'

'We try to make life easier for them, to make life, in so far as that is possible, even enjoyable.' He spoke the words with an almost devout dedication, as if he and his colleagues, in this isolated spot, were all too well aware of the ease with which a homeless, friendless, elderly, incurable refugee could be treated with only the minimum token respect for human dignity, and perhaps even less.

Certainly when we made a tour of the sanatorium later, the patients seemed to be sitting about the bright, spacious rooms or patrolling the long, polished corridors as if they could still hardly believe that all this was just for them. One or two even jumped exaggeratedly to attention to say good afternoon to the doctor as we passed. One man followed us for a while, chuckling to himself, and at one glass doorway the doctor, after peering in over our shoulders, hurriedly turned us away, saying philosophically: 'I shall just have to hope that that woman at the table didn't see you. It will mean a terrible time for me; she'll think I've brought the police to spy on her.'

He explained how most of the mental patients in the sanatorium were refugees who had suffered at the hands of the political police in the countries from which they had escaped.

'Their internal sense of persecution has followed them here, so that they live in a continuous state of terror and anxiety. They are unable to grasp that the police have not followed them here. They complain to me. Yes, I hope that woman didn't see you.'

He told us of another woman, a Hungarian in her forties, who had been arrested before the Hungarian rising of 1956. After a time in prison, during which she was interrogated about a resistance group to which her father was alleged to belong and of which she knew nothing, she was told one morning that she was going to be taken to see her father hanged. She still had nothing to tell. She was taken to a courtyard, where from a distance she saw a man hanged by the particularly brutal Hungarian method of garrotting on a post. A few days later she was told that the man whom she had seen hanged was not in fact her father, but that her father would be hanged if she didn't reveal what she knew about the resistance group. She knew nothing. Again she was taken to the courtyard and witnessed the hanging of a man she believed to be her father. But again the final torture was in reserve for her. Some time later she was taken to a room where an elderly man who had been stripped stark naked was being flogged round the room on all fours. A heavy stone had been suspended from his testicles. It was her father. He implored her to tell all she knew, but—and this possibly was the worst torture of all—she knew nothing. Shortly afterwards she had gone out of her mind. And although she had been rescued from prison after the 1956 rising she was still out of her mind in Thalham Sanatorium.

'They tell me endlessly, endlessly of such things. It is their only hope of recovery.' He paused and fixed me with his steely spectacles. 'You know, sometimes I ask myself, Herr Kee, whether the people who do such things to their fellow men can really be sane at all.'

I stared back at him.

Another type of mental case common among refugees was that of 'Occupation: Refugee. . . .' 'Such people, Herr Kee, make absolutely no attempt to adapt themselves to their new environment. They won't even speak German. . . .'

He agreed, however, with the High Commissioner's Mental Health Adviser's conclusions that on the whole it was the people who were unstable already who found refugee camps psychologically most disturbing. Those with no history of earlier psychological trauma were often left astonishingly undamaged by even the most adverse circumstances.

We crossed a quiet plot of grass to the tuberculosis centre, followed by curious eyes from the windows of the rooms we had just visited. As the doctor told us of his cases it became clear that there was another disease besides tuberculosis from which his patients were suffering: the indifference of the civilized world. He gave us clinical details.

A tubercular Yugoslav woman who had responded to the treatment in the sanatorium had now been negative for

four years. All this time she had been trying without success
to emigrate to the United States.

'While such people are sick, there is a nominal conscience about them. This fine sanatorium is built to look
after them. But when it achieves its object and cures them,
the world has no use for them. This is inhuman—*unmen-
schlich.*'

He cited a case of a twenty-eight-year-old Ukrainian who
had suffered for nine years from so-called 'traumatic'
tuberculosis.

'This is not inheritable, and, of course, it is the possible
inheritance of tuberculosis which makes immigration
authorities so strict about the disease. This Ukrainian's
parents have been living in the United States all these nine
years, but he is quite unable to join then. He will only be
able to join them if a special law is passed by Congress
permitting him to enter the States. The law, you see, as it
stands is quite ignorant of modern medicine.'

We were to see the Ukrainian later, accidentally, as he
stared at us from a window of the main block. There was a
vacant, almost happy expression of mild curiosity on this
face as if he had long forgotten why he was there.

We looked into a ward in which two young Albanians
and two young Yugoslavs were waiting patiently for their cure.

'But what is to happen to them when their wait is over?'
asked the doctor. 'Tuberculosis is a curable disease now.
But sometimes, with refugees, it seems as if the world finds
the consequences of this great achievement disagreeable.'

We walked into his consulting-room, and he rang a bell
for the Matron.

'I would like you to talk to a young man whom we have
cured here,' he said to us.

He came in a few minutes later, a young Hungarian of
twenty, rather short, with an almost gangling, resentful
gait. He had fine dark hair, brushed back, and an intelligent,
sensitive, but angry young face. He had escaped from
Hungary alone, a little after the Rising, on 27 December
1956. His name was Alexander Sirtes. He had been admitted to the sanatorium suffering from tuberculosis in

February 1958 and had been cured in September 1959. Ever since then he had been hanging about the sanatorium, vainly hoping to emigrate to the United States and growing more and more bitter every month. He had an aunt and a cousin already in the United States, but that had been no help to him.

'Have I got to hang around here until I become mentally ill to justify my existence?' he asked me angrily. I was the representative of the outside world, and he was wasting no time in letting me know what he thought of it.

I could see that already an unnatural, obsessional sense of persecution was present in his mind. Perhaps he could see this too, and it was this that gave added ferocity, bordering on frenzy, to his remark.

'But Sweden will take people with a T.B. history,' I said to him. 'Couldn't you go there instead?'

'I only want to go to America,' he said curtly. To him it was now an insult to suggest that he might have to compromise on the country of his choice. 'If I can't go there, I'll stay in Austria.'

I asked what profession he wanted to take up.

'Radio technician,' he answered, also curtly, as if I might be going to ask him to compomise on that too.

Once, he said, he'd been to Salzburg to be examined by a medical commission. He had sat about there all day and had come away fairly certain that 'they' hadn't even looked at his lung photograph.

'Well,' I said feebly, 'if you're determined it must be the United States, you must go on hoping. I'm sure you'll succeed in the end. You mustn't lose hope.'

So far he had grimly managed to control his anger. Now he gave up.

'Hope?' he spat out contemptuously. I could see the strain in the tendons of his neck. 'Hope! Hope! People always say to me I must hope. But what can hope mean after months and months of this?'

I saw that he was near to tears. For the first time I remembered that he was hardly more than a boy.

As we walked back towards our car the doctor said:

'It is of the utmost importance that there should be an absence of psychological upset in recovery from T.B. cases. Five times at least in the last nine months I have met that boy terribly depressed—so that I am beginning to worry about him. People are not objects which one can just leave lying about. You can leave things lying about, but not people. Something happens to them.'

He still spoke in the same quiet voice in which he had recounted the horrors of the Hungarian secret police.

'This must all be seen from the point of view of human dignity,' he went on. 'And although I am an Austrian myself I must say that the greater nations have something very simple to learn from Austria. Does Austria set up commissions on the frontiers to ask if these people have tuberculosis or any other "disqualification" when they come in?' He paused, a small, white figure with the wind mildly stirring the thin hair above his little spectacles. 'Here at the end of World Refugee Year these regulations disqualify people as human beings. This must not be. We must not tolerate the concept of the mass where people are concerned. The ninety-year-old grandmother who is completely off her head—and we have such people here— is someone whom we must treat as if she were our own, a most treasured person. *Es handelt sich um jeden einzelnen Mensch.* It's a matter of every single individual human being.'

He made it sound like a battle cry, and it was as if the greatest battle of all time was at stake.

He watched us go. He was standing there still, a movingly isolated figure in his white overalls, as we drove out onto the main road and out of sight.

Bill McCoy and I didn't talk much on the rest of the journey to Salzburg. Once, perhaps to keep my sympathies in perspective, he told me about a refugee, rejected for Canada, who had been given a flat with a low rent through U.S.E.P. The rent was low because U.S.E.P. had paid a lump sum down in advance, a sort of premium conferring the chief tenancy, or *Hauptmieterschaft*. But the original Canadian decision had later been reversed and the refugee had

K*

decided to emigrate. It was then that '. . . this codger was caught trying to flog the *Hauptmieterschaft*.'

When we got to Salzburg, Bill McCoy's concern for impartiality made him take me not only to the fine new apartment blocks put up with assistance from High Commissioner's funds at Taxham, where a flamboyant display of gaily-coloured balconies flashed like flags in the sun; not only to other blocks being completed in the Bessarabia Street, where small children of the families who had just moved in had the best of both worlds, playing old games in the camp-like wastes of the uncompleted new site; but also to the desolate shell of human habitation that was the withered remnant of Camp Parsch.

There were plenty of children here, too, making the most of the new space surprisingly bequeathed to them by the clearance of the old rotten barracks. In one of those that had not been cleared I paid the last call of my journey—on the Kulikovskis, an elderly Polish-Ukrainian couple who had been living there for the past nine years.

Sometime around Christmas they hoped to be moving into a new apartment in a block built with composite funds of the World Council of Churches and the High Commissioner for Refugees. They had already been to see the apartment in its half-completed form. But they were long past feelings of relief or even particular gratitude. I remembered what the doctor at Thalham had said so simply:

'You can't just leave human beings lying about as if they were objects. Something will happen to them.'

Not that the Kulikovskis were in any way ungracious. Like all refugees, they showed us great courtesy and civility. Surrounded by their elaborate, hand-embroidered cushions, and with Mr. Kulikovski's guitar hanging on the wall behind him (he had been a professional musician in the Ukraine before the war), they faced us across the table and honestly told us how they felt. And it was clear that in one way, after nearly twenty years in Austria, relief had come too late.

'Of course, it will be better to live in the new apartment like a man and a woman instead of like cattle in a stable, but . . . Well, in the first place, it will not be too pleasant moving in the middle of the winter, and there will be extra costs for us, such as heating and electricity, even though we won't have to pay the rent. It may not seem much extra to you, but our pension is 849 schillings (about £12) a month, and of this we reckon 120 schillings (about £1. 15s. 0d.) will be additional household costs.

'Both of us suffer from stomach trouble, so we have to buy as much fresh food as possible, which, of course, is very expensive. I would try to earn more money by taking light work if I could, but this sort of work is almost impossible to get if you're not an Austrian—it's only heavy, labouring jobs that you can pick up easily.'

(For a moment I had an uneasy memory of the old Czech couple who had walked out of Communist Czechoslovakia because the authorities had tried to suggest that they should do heavy work to keep alive.)

'But it's not only that. . . . This new apartment block we're going into . . . It's really just like a large barrack only better built. There will be fifty apartments there, all lived in by refugees. . . .'

'The corridors,' said Mrs. Kulikovski suddenly, 'are long corridors just like in the barracks, except that they are stone. . . . And, of course, the people who drank and shouted here will be drinking and shouting there too. . . . These refugee organizations know perfectly well who drinks and misbehaves and who doesn't. Why do they go on mixing us all up together?'

Her husband said calmly: 'What I should have liked would have been to have had a small house. It wouldn't have mattered how small. Just two little rooms and a separate kitchen. That's still my dream. A garden of course, would be too much to expect—a luxury even. . . .'

As so often on this journey, I was left speechless by my sense of inadequacy.

'Of course, I know what you could say,' said Mr. Kulikovski. 'You could say: Why don't we accept places in old people's homes? Well, I'll tell you. First, if we did so we'd lose our pension, because everything would be provided for in the home. But, secondly, every second of every day and night I would be reminded by being there that I was going to die. Of course, everyone knows he's going to die. But nobody knows when, and he can forget about it. In one of those places you would never be able to forget about it. By their very nature they're a sort of museum. They can't help being that. But I'm not going to be an exhibit in one.'

In the corridor as we made our way out I saw that the damp cardboard walls were full of holes, as if huge rats had been gnawing at them. Perhaps they had. A new motor-bicycle stood propped up incongruously in the darkness half-way down. It seemed an affront to the machine to keep it there.

For the last time in my life, I hope, I walked out of one of these evil places on which had been laid the seemingly undying curse of Hitler's Third Reich.

CONCLUSION

I had begun by thinking that the problem—the remains at least of this problem in Europe—could be cleared up quickly if tackled rightly. I ended by thinking that time and death alone would clear it up. I felt overwhelmed not so much by the refugee situation itself as by the human situation of which it was a symptom.

Somewhere between these two attitudes one must strike a balance.

In the modern world, refugees and bureaucratic lethargy are both aspects of the human condition, like suffering and ugliness. Another aspect of the human condition is the need to fight against the evil it envolves. If, in this account of the refugee situation in Austria and Germany at the end of World Refugee Year. I have concentrated on failure rather than success, it is because I wanted to stress the difficulty and complicated nature of the fight even in this small corner of the refugee field. And the refugee field is in its turn only one corner of the whole field of human suffering.

World Refugee Year itself was a great attempt to draw attention to a world situation which had been shamefully neglected. How much of a success has it been?

Perhaps its most important objective was simply to bring about this increased awareness of what needed to be done. In this it has undoubtedly been a success. But how lasting is the nature of this increased awareness going to be?

In practical terms, World Refugee Year has successes to record. But it must also be recorded that they are limited. And perhaps at this stage it is again of more value to stress the limitations than the success.

The total additional amount of money contributed for refugees in World Refugee Year was about £30,000,000. One-quarter of this was subscribed by the British people.[1] These sums were, of course, collected for all refugees all

[1] The total figure for contributions from the United Kingdom was roughly £8,000,000. The Government share of this was £400,000.

over the world: not only for the estimated 110,000 unsettled 'mandate' refugees in Europe (of whom only those in
Germany and Austria have been the subject of this report),
but also for the 250,000 (mostly women and children) in
Tunisia and Morocco, for the 1,120,000 in Palestine (half
of whom are under fifteen), for the 2,500,000 in Pakistan,[2]
the 4,000,000 in Korea and 1,000,000 in Hong Kong.[3]

Taking money as a symbol of felt obligation and responsibility, this £30,000,000 does not seem a figure of
which eighty countries, representing 800,000,000 people,
can feel particularly proud, though relatively the British
people and the people of the Scandinavian countries,
especially Norway, whose contributions were also dis-
proportionately high, obviously have their own reasons for
pride. But it should be remembered that, for instance, the
British alone contribute to their own Health Service over
£600,000,000 a year.

In what other ways has the world's new awareness and
sense of responsibility for refugees shown itself? Again
we can take Europe as a small but useful example. The
greatest cause for congratulation has been the partial
relaxation by some governments of their rigid immigration
laws. But an examination in detail of the progress achieved
serves rather to highlight the shamefulness of the past
than the generosity of the present. Between 1952 and
1959 only 4,665 'handicapped' refugees out of a largely
'handicapped' total of 300,000 were resettled, and 2,826 of
these were taken by Sweden.[4] Thus it is now cause for
congratulations when, as happened in World Refugee Year,
the United Kingdom produces a scheme for the admission
of 1,000 sponsored refugees and 210 suffering from dis-
abilities such as tuberculosis; or Canada a scheme for
100 refugee families, each with a member suffering from

[2] There are also an estimated 2,500,000 Hindu and Sikh refugees in
India, but the Government of India does not recognize them as having
any special refugee status, regarding them merely as Indian citizens.

[3] See Appendix A.

[4] The rest had gone mainly to Belgium, France, Denmark, Switzerland,
Norway, and the Netherlands.

active tuberculosis; Australia a scheme for 500 refugee families; New Zealand one for 140; Sweden another one for 350 'handicapped' refugees; Norway another for 100 tubercular cases and the United States provides for the admission of 500 'difficult to resettle' cases.

But Norway and Sweden, it might be argued, had already produced more than their share of such schemes. Together with the British people's justifiable self-congratulation on their achievement should go the reminder that between 1952 and 1959 only sixty-four 'handicapped' refugees were admitted to the United Kingdom and those all in 1956, the year of the Hungarian rising.

And the dismal fact remains that, in a World Refugee Year called after nine years of neglect, the 'have' countries of the United Nations were unable to share out between them, without criteria or qualifications of any sort, the relatively few remaining handicapped and unhandicapped refugees in Europe who wished to be resettled.

There have been other practical successes of a sort in World Refugee Year. The Office of the High Commissioner for Refugees set itself as No. 1 target for World Refugee Year: camp clearance in Europe. If you can regard as 'camp clearance' the drawing up of the *plans* for camp clearance and the securing of funds to implement those plans then the target was achieved. Little true clearance was achieved. As this book has shown, there were thousands of refugees in camps in Austria and Germany alone for whom World Refugee Year made no difference at all. During the year the 'mandate' camp population in Europe actually fell by *less* than it had fallen in the previous six months—from 23,520 to 17,330, compared with from 32,000 to 23,520.[5] The Director of the Office of the High Commissioner for Refugees, who gives these figures, comments publicly: 'All mandate refugees should now know, however, that the end of their ordeal is in sight, and that they will soon be given

[5] These figures are given by Thomas Jamieson, Director of the Office of the High Commissioner for Refugees, Geneva, on p. 9. of the November–December issue of *Migration News*, published by the Intertional Catholic Migration Commission in Geneva.

the opportunity of living a normal life and becoming permanently settled in their community.' With some knowledge of an internal and external refugee world that has lasted for fifteen years, it is difficult to read such words without impatience.

For the out-of-camp mandate refugees the Director has not even this cold comfort. 'The sum of $6,570,000 was earmarked', he writes, 'to make a start during 1960 towards finding permanent solutions for the out-of-camp refugees, priority being given to handicapped refugees. Unfortunately, in this field, it was possible to raise only less than half the sum.'

Judging again from the particular standpoint of the European refugee situation, one feels compelled to ask whether the available machinery for dealing with it is suitably competent. Broadly speaking, this machinery consists of the following organizations: (1) the under-financed United Nations refugee organization, the Office of the High Commissioner for Refugees; (2) about eighty 'voluntary agencies', of which four are by far the most powerful—the World Council of Churches, the National Catholic Welfare Conference, the Lutheran World Federation and the American Joint Distribution Committee;[6] (3) the International Committee for European Migration; and (4)—tangential to the above three elements, because self-contained, whereas they are all to a certain extent interdependent; the United States Escapee Programme.

That excellent work has been done and is being done by all these organizations is undeniable. That the effectiveness of this machinery is proportionate to its immense cost and complexity is less certain—particularly if one remembers that the European refugee situation, in this form, has lasted for nine years and is so relatively small. I cannot forget the head of the United Ukrainian Relief Committee, who said to me that the small British Adoption Committee for

---

[6] Other important 'voluntary agencies' are: the Friends World Committee, the International Rescue Committee—first in the field, in time—, the International Social Service, and the International Catholic Migration Commission.

Displaced Persons, with its principle of direct action and absence of red tape, had done more for his refugees than all the other organizations put together. Nor can I forget the Pumyczs in the Moosacherstrasse, or the Romaniszins in Malmsheim, or Alexander Terlecki and family in Bad Cannstast, or Mehmed Karmovi in Valka, or the Arnautovic family in Asten, or the people in Unterjettingen, or the Kulikovskis in Camp Parsch or any of them.

I cannot forget that I met them after the end of World Refugee Year in Europe in July 1960.

And when I remember them and remember with them the 'new' refugees, the young Jugoslav families and single boys waiting for months on end at Traiskirchen, I cannot forget an interview with a deeply disturbed official of the International Committee for European Migration which I had in Salzburg a few hours before I returned to London.

'We have money this year,' he told me, 'and transport facilities to move 8,000 people of whom 6,000 can be refugees. So far we have only received for movement 1,756 people, of whom 1,080 are refugees. Even granted that there are another five months of the year to go, this is way behind our capability. For instance, between April and September of this year we were committed to and able to move 500 people a month to Canada. We have been moving only between fifty and seventy a month. . . . I cannot judge about what is happening in other stages of the European refugee field. All I can tell you is that there are 1,000 refugees hanging around for months in Traiskirchen, and yet I cannot fill my ships. . . . We at I.C.E.M. are not getting the people for movement.'

What I can forget is the interview I had a few weeks later with the High Commissioner for Refugees himself. A charming, energetic, pipe-smoking Swiss who spoke perfect English, he met all my criticisms and queries with a tolerant sympathy and concern. He left me with the feeling that if we hadn't exactly solved the world's refugee problems together, we had examined them thoroughly in a quite un-bureaucratic way, and found that though, regretfully, progress was slow, it wasn't for want of effort on the part of decent, hard-working people like himself and his staff. A short time later this well-liked able personality was promoted Swiss Ambassador to Washington. And the Pumyczs, the Romaniszins, the Terleckis, and the rest were put under the 'mandate' of a new High Commissioner.

It isn't good enough. But what can be done?

In Europe there are two practical steps which could, if energetically carried out, clear all camps and solve most out-of-camp refugees' problems within a matter of weeks. They could have been carried out any time in the last nine years. It is even easier to carry them out now.

(1) For those refugees who still wish to emigrate, all immigration criteria should be waived immediately by an agreed number of governments able to share out the relatively small intake between them. This would inevitably involve accepting a few, but only a very few, refugees to be supported on the public charge. The vast majority of refugees would soon be able to support themselves, and it would be the job of voluntary agencies and committees to enable them to do so and to keep a watching eye on them. Even those refugees who could not support themselves would often bring children who would soon become assets to their foster-mother country, like the Bulgarian-Polish couple to whom Watson introduced me in the Schleissheimerstrasse in Munich.[7] As to the very few who would be a charge on the State, a civilization which boasts as much as ours does of its belief in the dignity of the individual should be proud to be able to pay this small tribute to its ideal—if not as an outright tribute, then at least in expiation for the neglect of the past.

If governments still feel unable to carry out such a radical measure—and democratic governments will in fact do anything their people press them to do hard enough—then at least, when applying immigration criteria, their missions should visit refugees in camps and make direct personal contact with them. This may cost more time and money, but again, if the public feels its responsibility strongly

[7] See Chapter IV.

enough, it will give its government the money to discharge it.

(2) For those refugees who wish to remain in their countries of first asylum—and this, after so many years, now probably means the majority, whatever their former wishes—the slow, long-term, ultra-economic planning of housing becomes even more anachronistic with every additional day that passes. After so many years of neglect, immediate action is automatically the best. In Germany and Austria every effort should now be concentrated on securing small existing apartments with rents made tolerable for refugees, by means of a lump sum payment of key money. For an average apartment today this would work out at around £350. *Per capita* it may, of course, be a more expensive way of housing refugees than the present careful economic methods, which are competent except that they house refugees so slowly. But it should not be difficult to persuade governments that, though literally more expensive, this is the most truly economical way of settling the problem. Not only does it settle it once and for all, but, given the wish to help refugees at all, the invisible cost of making a refugee who has already waited fifteen years wait another year or even three months is incalculable. The longer the ordeal, the more intolerable the delay, not vice versa.

An objection to this scheme, apart from the additional cost, is made, first, on the grounds that there simply wouldn't be a sufficient number of apartments available, and, secondly, that such a large sudden demand would force up prices. But the purchase of apartments is the normal method of acquiring them on the German and Austrian market. The addition of a few thousand more to the demand would make little appreciable difference to what is already such a large market. The still relatively low average price of £350 proves that the demand is by no means excessive. A great deal of hard work would have to be done in the real estate market, but a great deal of hard work is being done for refugees, anyway. Operations would be just switched to a more effective field.

But the gross cost *might* be considerably more than at

present and this is where, again, the private individual comes in. The very first step of all in solving this or any other refugee problem must be an increase in each private individual's sense of responsibility. The individual must feel the positive need not only to share more of his relative wealth in the form of private charity, if that is the way he likes to do it—but also, and this technically is the easier though clumsier way—to pay more in the form of taxes, so that his government can confer on him the dignity of discharging his responsibility for him.

Only 130 years ago, when the Industrial Revolution was getting into its stride, the new industrial societies of Western Europe, but particularly Britain, contained conditions of poverty, misery, hardship, and squalor comparable to, and in some ways worse than, the conditions in which most refugees and the inhabitants of the 'underdeveloped' countries of the world live today. At first private charity took on almost the entire responsibility for dealing with these conditions. But gradually individuals put pressure on governments to discharge their human responsibility for them. One has only to glance through a few pages of the British Government's inquiries into the working and living conditions of the 19th century poor to be astonished by the toleration of such inhumanity within a society that was in its fundamental outlook both humane and civilized. Such conditions existed, in fact, side by side with great culture and comfortable living in exactly the same way as today the culture and comfortable living of the majority of Western Europe exists side by side with the inhumanity of conditions elsewhere in the world, and even in some corners of Europe itself. Private individuals, even those who took little active part in charity, must have been continually distressed and confused by their own feelings of helplessness and their incapacity to do anything about such conditions, in much the same way as many people today feel distressed about refugees and others suffering from indescribable hardship. In many ways it must have been a relief when governments began to assume the responsibility in the individual's name. For it is, of course, the proper function of government to assume the burden of moral obligation when this is too considerable or complicated for the individual to discharge himself.

The idea of social justice has developed rapidly in the last 130 years and particularly in Britain during the last 15, so that a term like 'the welfare state', which was once used as a political gibe, has in general come to be accepted as a desirable common objective. The world problem of social justice is only beginning to be recognized—and mainly by the United States of America—and the real development is still to come.

Of course, no refugee problem can, in the end, be separated from the larger problem of the world's poverty, hunger, and misery as a whole. Indeed, a terrifying illustration of this is found in the fact that in many parts of the world the distribution of temporary relief to refugees causes a new social problem of its own. Refugees who have been given what the Western world considers the indispensable basic minimum necessary for the dignity and survival of a human being become privileged persons among the local population. This applies not only to India, Pakistan, Korea, and Palestine, but also to parts of Greece and Italy as well. And in one sense it is true that the refugee is a privileged person. He is privileged inasmuch as political events have drawn the world's attention to his misery slightly more than to the misery of millions of other human beings which is forgotten about or taken for granted.

If then an attempt were made to tackle the world refugee problem properly for the first time, it could be as a first battle in a greater campaign. And with this campaign our civilization—in spite of the moss eaten off the rocks in Korea, in spite of the misery of Bad Cannstast or Karachi— might still become what it is so obviously capable of being: the most marvellous in the history of man.

APPENDIX A

Apart from the refugee situations already mentioned, there have been two other major refugee problems since the war: the 400,000 Finns from the Karelian isthmus which was ceded to Russia after the war, and the 1,000,000 or so refugees from North Vietnam who poured into South Vietnam after the partition of that country in 1955. The Finns have been completely successfully integrated, the Vietnamese—with U.S. help—largely so. The South Vietnamese Government refrained from asking for help during World Refugee Year.

Other refugee groups in the world include 20,000 Tibetans in Nepal and Sikkim; 40,000 Chinese on the Portuguese island of Macao, and—included among 200,000 Dutch 'national' refugees from Indonesia—25,000 Amboynese in Holland. There are also some 7,000 European refugees in Communist China—mainly White Russians and former anti-Nazis—who are under the mandate of the High Commissioner, and are slowly being evacuated with the agreement of the Communist Chinese Government.

In Europe, in addition to the refugees in Germany, Austria and Holland, there are:

In *France*: some 40,000 refugees who lead a 'precarious existence', according to the French World Refugee Year Committee. They are mainly White Russians and Spanish Republicans. None lives in camps.

In *Italy*: 6,000 foreign refugees in five camps and 3,000 more non-settled foreign refugees living outside camps. In addition, of the estimated 400,000 'national' refugees from Venezia Giulia, Egypt, and North Africa, 20,000 are living in camps and another 20,000 in conditions of grave need outside camps (figures for 30 April 1960).

In *Greece*: 800 mandate refugees in camps and a further 9,000 'in dire need of assistance'. There is also a large undetermined number of 'national' refugees in need, some of whom have been refugees for nearly forty years (figures for October 1959).

The total number of refugees in the whole world is sometimes given as 40,000,000, but this is misleading, since the figure includes 'settled' refugees.

All refugees figures should be treated with great reserve and regarded only as rough pointers to a situation.

APPENDIX B

A few of the organizations working for refugees:
The United Nations High Commissioner for Refugees
Main office
Palais des Nations
Geneva, Switzerland
> Branch offices,
>> Germany:
>> Remigisstrasse, 5
>> Bonn
>> Austria:
>>> Opernring I, Stiege E/5
>>> Opernringhof
>>> Vienna. I

World Council of Churches
17 Route de Malagnou
Geneva. Switzerland

The National Catholic Welfare Conference
11 rue de Cornavin
Geneva. Switzerland

Lutheran World Federation
17 Route de Malagnou
Geneva. Switzerland

League of Red Cross Societies
17 Chemin des Crets
Petit Saconnex, Geneva. Switzerland
> (The principal agency concerned with refugees in Tunisia
> and Morocco)

In Britain:
Lifeline (formerly The British Adoption Committee for Aid
> to Displaced Persons)
67A Camden High Street
London. NW1

British Council for Aid to Refugees
9 Grosvenor Crescent, London. SW1

Oxford Committee for Famine Relief
17 Broad Street
Oxford

Printed in Great Britain by
The Camelot Press Ltd., London and Southampton